Doing the Needful

Doing the Needful

The Dilemma of India's Population Policy

G. Narayana
and John F. Kantner

Routledge
Taylor & Francis Group

NEW YORK AND LONDON

First published 1992 by Westview Press, Inc.

Published 2021 by Routledge
605 Third Avenue, New York, NY 10017
2 Park Square, Milton Park, Abingdon, Oxon OX14 4RN

Routledge is an imprint of the Taylor & Francis Group, an informa business

Copyright © 1992 by Taylor & Francis

Library of Congress Cataloging-in-Publication Data
Narayana, G.
  Doing the Needful : The Dilemma of India's Population
Policy / G. Narayana, John F. Kantner
    p. cm.
Includes bibliographical references and index.
ISBN 0-8133-8432-X
1. Birth control—India. 2. Birth control—
Government policy—India. 3. India—population
policy. I. Kantner, John Frederick, 1920–
II.Title.
HQ766.5.I5N283 1992
363. 9′6′0954—dc20

                                        91-23370
                                        CIP

ISBN 13: 978-0-3670-1142-0 (hbk)
ISBN 13: 978-0-3671-6129-3 (pbk)

DOI: 10.4324/9780429041280

Contents

Tables

Preface

At the moment of the long awaited "tryst with destiny," as Prime Minister Nehru announced the advent of an Independent India, there were less than 350 million Indians to share the exhilaration of that midnight hour. Since then much has happened. Some hopes have been fulfilled; perhaps more have been denied. The nation stands in great peril, both for the sanctity of its democratic institutions and processes and for the unity of its culturally diverse parts.

Today there are half a billion or so more Indians than were present at the nation's birth. For many, life chances have improved but the "poor" in present day India are almost as numerous as the entire population at the time of the last pre-Independence Census.

Independent India has had a troubled history. While it has made it through some difficult times, the problems now confronting the country are as serious as any in its short history. Unless these are solved, the result could be the abrogation of the democratic principles which this nation, more than almost any other new nation of the modern period, has struggled to preserve. And yet many who know India have faith that as the old order passes, as it surely will, the resolve to survive without overturning the institutions and values that India takes as its heritage will come forward and prevail. But like a sack full of writhing cobras, religious bigotry, caste conflict, political pandering and posturing, corruption and unenlightened, unbridled self interest threaten to break through a dangerously threadbare social fabric. A favorable outcome cannot be taken for granted.

India's dilemma is that the things it must do to save itself as a unified and democratic nation frequently run counter to the deep seated, conflicting interests of obdurate and powerful constituencies. The result is paralysis of political decision and a neutralized bureaucracy.

A chorus of intellectuals deplores and excoriates these practices but to little effect. The "great souls" that occasionally appear, meteor-like in this darkening sky, raise one's gaze to higher possibilities but have not, since Gandhiji's time, been able to summon the mass of the people to greater purpose. In these respects India is not different from other diverse and troubled nations that seek to orchestrate their differences through a functioning system of governance.

This book is not about anything so broad as the health of Indian society. It deals instead with a particular problem, the problem of rapid population growth, that makes India's transition to a post-agrarian order more difficult than it might otherwise be. Population growth is not India's most troubling problem, at least not in the short run. It is one, however, that must be addressed—and in a more effective manner than so far has been the case. And so the book is about the nature of those efforts, the reasons they have not been more successful and how they might be improved.

A major theme of what is written here is the pervasive nature of the failures that have beset India's interventions in the social service area and the commonality of the approaches that have led to those failures. While many have made suggestions toward better policy and improved programs—and we do so here also—the problem lies in large part beyond the reach of particular program modifications. What is required is a reorientation of policy, a redirection of effort, a "basic overhaul" of administration and fundamental change in attitudes and relationships throughout the systems whereby the society (we do not say, merely, "the government") looks out for its welfare. We do not have the answers to all of the questions we shall raise. We do present ideas, not all of them new or original, that represent breaks with past approaches and promising avenues of advance toward a future in which the nation can invest more in the quality of its people and less in paying the costs of excess numbers.

G. Narayana
John F. Kantner

Acknowledgments

Of the many persons who have helped us in putting this book together—some knowingly, others not—we wish to give special thanks to Mike Jordan, who commissioned the original effort as a primer on India's population problem for the USAID India Mission. No doubt he did not expect to be taken so seriously and no doubt he will find that much of what is written here exceeds the purposes he had in mind. We are indebted also to Owen Cylke, somewhat a rarity among Mission Directors, who, against a strong bureaucratic undertow, encouraged his staff to know India and to think creatively about a proper and effective role for US foreign assistance.

We must praise tolerance and forbearance in other places also. Our parent institutions, The Administrative Staff College of India and the Johns Hopkins University, accommodated our respective absences graciously. And one of us must pay tribute to the farsighted but to us unknown souls who invented the Joint Career Corps as a means of bringing about closer contact between academe and government service. Their idea is little more than a dinghy among the large bottoms of the US foreign assistance establishment, but dinghies have their uses.

Thanks are due the Rockefeller Foundation for a grant that helped with some of our expenses. That august institution has a long history of service to the people of India. It is the kind of organization that can still play a small but significant role in releasing the best impulses and energies of our two countries in a joint search for better understanding and mutuality of purpose.

Finally, we are extremely grateful to Mr. S. B. Mishra, Joint Secretary (Policy), and Mr. R. L. Narasimhan, Director (Evaluation), for their encouragement and for their comments on the Indian Population Control Programme. Our criticisms of the Indian bureaucracy in general and the Ministry of Health and Family Welfare in particular should be leavened by the recognition of the many dedicated professionals within the system who, paraphrasing former Justice Thurgood Marshall, do the best they can with what they have to work.

G.N.

J.F.K.

1

Indian Society on the Threshold of the 21st Century

Social Transition

India, not yet the world's largest country, is on its way to becoming so. In itself that achievement will have little meaning although when and, it must be said, if, it happens, much will be made of it. Even now, however, striking comparisons can be drawn to underscore the fact of India's demographic preeminence. As Frank Hobbs (Hobbs, 1986) once noted, India has more people than all of Africa, more than North and South America together and is approximately equal in size to the combined populations of Europe and the Soviet Union.

Size is undeniably important but of greater significance is what India represents in the world "community" of nations and what it might be in the future. However troubled and divided—and despite occasional lapses into nondemocratic ways—India stands out among less developed nations of substantial size as one that is attempting to modernize itself, socially and economically, without sacrificing its commitment to democratic processes. Certainly, there have been periods of crisis and emergency when the government has turned more high-handed and arbitrary than is consistent with its sense of its better self. And there is still much social disenfranchisement, mistrust of the organs of justice, denial of opportunity, intolerance, infringement of rights, corruption, violence and other signs of institutional immaturity in this still young nation. A nation, it might be said, with steadier and nobler aspirations for itself and its people than most post colonial societies.

India is a country bursting with diversity. It has only a nascent cohesiveness beyond the bounds and bonds of kin and caste and is relatively new to the ways of democratic self rule. Despite (some would say be-

1

cause of) severe internal strains and stresses India at times assumes external responsibilities that derive from and are commensurate with its size and position. It has asserted a hegemonic claim to involvement in the affairs of the volatile Indian Ocean region, an involvement which may have ended the political dominance of the Nehru dynasty. It has sought to be a factor in bringing stability and moderation to the political expression of Islamic fundamentalism in Northwest Asia. In addition, among the aspiring nations that as a "nonaligned" block have tried to leverage world affairs in their favor, India has pressed a sometimes sullied but, nevertheless, unrivaled suit for leadership. India, in short, is a world force, if not yet a fully accredited world power.

India's past and potential contributions to art, science and to the realm of the unknowable, are immense. It is one of the world's great cultural granaries. And it is a nation of great promise in science, the arts, philosophy, and in material achievement. Though its lamp often sputters, it may yet become a beacon for nations seeking a non-authoritarian path to development. The experience of other large, complex societies would suggest that the potential of this highly textured, deeply rooted, society will be realized in fullest measure if it remains open to change, frees itself from the imperatives of unproductive economic and political doctrine and resists the calls of communal interests that now threaten its integrity as a unified nation. Much is at stake for India, for the region it dominates and for the rest of the world in India's attempt to negotiate the transition from a segmented, agrarian society, still considerably enmeshed in the bonds of feudalism, to an integrated, industrialized, urbanizing nation at relative peace with itself.

The problems that must be dealt with in order to secure India's future are both formidable and familiar. Most urgent, for the immediate future, is the problem of dissent and devolution. Minority populations (the term is relative, Muslims alone number 100 million) resist being dissolved, as they see it, in a Hindu melting pot. This is an old problem in India. In our time, the failure to accommodate the Muslim minority on terms acceptable to its leaders led to the preventable tragedy of Partition. The same kind of failure now fans the flames in Punjab, Kashmir and Assam.

The issues behind the social and political ferment in India today are not rooted primarily in economic deprivation and frustration though these make the mix more volatile. Rather it is the widespread feeling that the institutions on which the society was founded no longer work. The Delhi correspondent of the London *Economist* (*The Economist*, May 25st–31st, 1991) in a reflective piece written shortly after the assassination of Rajiv Gandhi observed that

The state is seen as corrupt and callous, incapable of delivering justice or prosperity to the people . . . The police and civil service are seen as oppressors and terrorists. The law courts are venal and can take decades to decide a case. The rule of law does not seem to work in settling people's grievances. What seems to work is violence and money, and all political parties are engaged in a mad race to maximize the use of both . . . Amid this moral decay, religious, ethnic and caste crusades have a growing appeal. People find a purity in them which they do not find in secular, national parties. And an increasing number of people are willing to kill in the name of causes which they find holier than the discredited law of the land.

The creed of Gandhi and Nehru which held that the country's cultural diversity must be accommodated in a secular democracy is under severe challenge. Hindu chauvinism, which under the aegis of the Bharatiya Janata Party (BJP) is making a strong bid for political and moral leadership, is a case in point. It (the BJP) offers the frustrated and confused members of the largest religious community moral certainty and emotional release in place of an aseptic secularism. More generally, when the center no longer inspires loyalties that go beyond particular communal boundaries and when there is no group so undebased by deals struck in the political market place that it can speak in the name of national unity, the way is open for demagogic appeals to sections of the population that seek security in a sea of change. They seek a more focussed cultural identity and a political base for protecting or advancing their claims against the larger society. Secularism cannot work without a strong center whose authority is conceded to be legitimate.

For India secularism was the path chosen by Nehru to avoid the "politicization of deep-rooted primordial loyalties" (Kohli, *World Development*, Mar. '89). To keep divisive communal loyalties permanently submerged, Nehru launched the nation on a course of socialist development which featured central planning, an emphasis on the public sector and programs of economic uplift for the poor. The implicit theory of the state under which Nehru's state guided capitalism proceeded was of the romantic variety: the state was assumed to be informed, competent in the exercise of its functions and committed to the promotion of the general welfare. Democracy was not a distant goal to be achieved upon a relaxation of the discipline demanded for development, but a condition given at the outset—the hallmark of the Indian way that distinguished it from the authoritarian course followed by its arch rival, China.

In reality, Indian democracy has often been more form than substance. As students of modernization generally agree, economic development in association with the elaboration of a market exchange economy is a prerequisite for true political democracy. Modernization also is thought to require an initial concentration and expansion of power necessary to contain and redirect the forces unleashed by the breakdown of traditional institutions and practices. Development can then be entrusted to a rational, secular, system of authority operating through an efficient, disinterested bureaucracy and protected from internal reaction and external exploitation by a professional, apolitical military. It is difficult while the voyage to modernization is in mid-passage to achieve more than a rudimentary expression of democracy. This is particularly so of the present era in which nation building has become a more hazardous undertaking than it was historically for Western countries.

Today most observers would likely reject the romantic version of the Indian state for a more cynical one that sees the state as predatory and incompetent in many of its actions. In this view, government efforts to direct the course of development produce unintended "distortions," its programs of economic and social reform tend to be ineffective and the selling of economic and political dispensations is a principal activity of the civil service.

The truth, as is usually the case, lies somewhere between these extreme views but there is little question that the image of the Indian state and its modes of operation has been badly tarnished since Nehru proclaimed the country's "tryst with destiny." Moreover, there is no consensus on what is needed to move the country ahead. Advocates of greater economic liberalization blame the economic controls generated by the policy of "self reliance" and socialist dogma for the relatively sluggish pace of development. Opponents of liberalization, which include most of the Congress rank and file, parties of the left and leaders with a rural constituency, argue that liberalization favors the business community and the urban middle class. The problem, they insist, is not controls but insufficient demand and neglect of public investment. What is needed, according to this diagnosis, is less urban bias in development policy and greater attention to investment and to policies favorable to agriculture. But, as Kohli has noted, a shifting of resources toward agriculture and away from industry and the urban middle could be dangerously disruptive of established state-society relationships and also risks getting mired down in intractable and politically dangerous issues like land reform (Kohli, op cit). The result has been a policy of deferral and muddle-through with a concomitant intensification of political jostling for power.

The problem remains, as one student of Indian society put it (Lannoy,

1975), of finding "new ways of positive pluralism" in which all groups can be accommodated. The most insistent political movements today— Hindu revivalism, secessionist and separatist violence, demands for and against caste-based job reservations—are at odds with this ideal. Also working against an accommodative pluralism is the electoral process, the DNA of a modern democratic state. In India caste, religion and class are exploited as instruments of political mobilization. Electoral politics thus keeps the cauldron of cultural antagonism bubbling. Except for periods of crisis, such as the break-up along religious lines at the time of Partition, India has managed so far to accommodate and contain the disruptive force latent in group differences. Today the workable accommodations that have permitted the country to deal with its diversity are under extreme pressure. Faced with threats of secession, caste warfare, and sectarian violence the temptation is to adopt stern measures in support of central authority. Such a course, which was the way of the Moguls toward the end of their reign (George, 1986), risks either the break-up of the nation or the denial of its basic values—or both.

It is commonplace to observe that the old order in rural India is breaking up. Oft cited evidence of this is the widespread abandonment and modification of the "jajmani" system that traditionally has regulated relationships between land owners and their laborers. Customary systems of rewards give way when new technologies and expanded market areas introduce a new calculus of advantage for those who control the scarce resources of the community. Innumerable studies of social and economic change in Indian villages illustrate this process (Epstein).

Related to the crumbling of the "cake of custom," are increasing challenges to the caste system as traditionally interpreted. The ambiguity of caste in occupational terms is the wedge by which the lower castes winkle their way upward on the scale, a process that Srinivas, the doyen of Indian anthropologists, has called "Sanskritisation." However the ambiguity is not so great as to render the system inoperative. Violations of caste norms, as for example intercaste marriage, still evoke responses of bestial ferocity. Educated Indians look upon such incidents as throwbacks to the inhumanity of feudal times that must be dealt with sternly by the authorities. But efforts to create greater equality of opportunity for members of the traditionally disadvantaged castes meet stiff resistance from these same ranks. Resistance ranges from pious insistence on meritocracy, which in a system rife with nepotism and corruption is a tarnished ideal, to violent protest. In some northern areas upper caste students have taken to the streets in protest over the reservation of government jobs for lower caste applicants, jobs that on the basis of educational qualification and influence would likely be theirs. The issue is undisguisedly one of caste rather than economic need since many of those who would benefit from the proposed reservation policy are not needy in the customary sense.

Religious intolerance is the second serious fault line in Indian society. Hindu-Muslim antagonism, which after Partition had lapsed into relative quiescence, has again become inflamed, this time with the demand for a final solution that would make the terms "Hindu" and "India" synonymous. The rhetoric is strident and uncompromising and recalls the insistence on "Aryan" purity of a different time and place. Hindu holy men have been summoned by the promoters of Hindu revivalism to abandon their otherworldly preoccupation and give their blessing to a politically ambitious, exclusionary, Hindu nationalism. Some have refused, saying that religion and politics are not to be mixed; many, however, have obliged, proclaiming that indeed the faith must be given political expression. Hinduism, traditionally a loosely structured, non-organized, individualistic faith with a choice of gods to worship, is now undertaking an earthly mission. Though the religious side (the VHP) and the political side (the BJP) are not yet at one, each insisting on its own separate organizational identity, Hindu nationalism is a gathering force of portentous proportion.

Theoretically, it might be supposed that Hindu chauvinism would dissolve inter-caste antagonism in a brew of fervid fundamentalism. This has not happened and it is unlikely that it will. The call for Hindu revival is not a call to Hindu brotherhood but a call to arms, literally and figuratively, against non-Hindus. The outlook is for continued and possibly intensified inter-caste violence as the Hindu "yatra" rolls on and as new outrages become old scores to be settled.

Religion is also a central factor in the secessionist strife in Punjab and Kashmir. Sikh terrorists in Punjab seek to frighten Hindus into leaving rural areas of the state and even the state itself. Should the tactic succeed and should Sikhs residing in other parts of India feel pressed by a Hindu backlash to join their co-religionists in Punjab, the claim for Sikh statehood would be strengthened. The principle of ethnic and linguistic homogeneity as justification for statehood has been recognized by past territorial reorganizations in India and thus it is not surprising that territorial demands based on cultural exclusiveness are still being pressed.

Secessionist sentiment is strong also in Kashmir which has a predominantly Muslim population. Many there want to join the Muslim world either as an independent state or as part of Pakistan. The softer option of autonomy within India has less appeal. Kashmir has great strategic,

economic and sentimental value for India and thus there is little likelihood that the secessionist's demands will be acceded to. The deadlock
between Delhi and Srinigar over what are essentially non-negotiable
positions seems destined to persist. Meanwhile the economy of Kashmir
which is based on tourism and the export of handicrafts, has come to a
standstill as the militant movement for azadi (freedom) and government
paramilitary forces, by threat and by curfew, have paralyzed such economic activity as has not already fled the area.

Throughout India, Muslim populations are devising new accommodations that they hope will permit them to survive as a loyal minority.
The secessionism of Kashmiri Muslims is based on the fact that they are
in the majority and is sustained by deeply believed allegations of
perfidious past treatment by Hindu dominated governments in Delhi.
Elsewhere in India Muslims are moving away from defiance and
belligerence toward accommodation based on professed loyalty to the
Indian state and support for secular solutions to the country's problems.
Some Muslim leaders nevertheless champion a fundamentalist Muslim
faith as the basis for communal identity, self respect and security.

Religion and caste are the primary, but not the sole, divisive forces in
Indian society. As the population of India has increased and become
more differentiated, politically charged differences based on class and
residence also have appeared. These crosscut but seldom override
differences based on caste and religion. Indeed attempts to unite prole-
tarian elements or to organize farmers to counter the alleged urban bias
in Indian development policy frequently fall apart along caste lines.

In the face of such divisive and centrifugal forces the Congress party
which once spoke commandingly with the voice of India, has lost its
sense of direction. In recent years it has hung by a dynastic thread
which has now been broken. The party, which more than forty years
ago set the country on a course of planned change under the mantle of a
serious but sedate socialism sponsored by an enlightened and accepted
leadership, is in relative disarray. Its actions in recent days are characterized more by manipulation and maneuver than by the purposeful
pursuit of articulated policy. Rajiv Gandhi's attempts on becoming
Prime Minister to put the country on a pragmatic path toward modernization did succeed in clearing away some administrative underbrush.
Policies were adopted that made it easier for firms to enter into production and to make their own decisions on what and how much to produce. Tariffs were substituted in some cases for import restrictions and
import barriers were lowered on selected items. Corporation and individual income taxes were lowered and some assurance was given to the
business community concerning levels of future taxation. Equally im-

portant, the government attempted in a forthcoming way to deal with separatist demands. But then it stopped. Economic policy retained its strong interventionist tendencies and moves toward accord on separatist issues were first delayed then deferred and eventually dropped altogether.

The Prime Minister scored his party for its failings and its faint-heartedness but could not, at least did not, revive his reform agenda to any significant degree. The Congress party became increasingly absorbed with the tactics of political survival and the keenest advocates of liberalization found themselves out of official favor. For most politicians, civil servants, and those in public sector corporations a serious threat to their way of life had blown over.

Since none of the parties that base their appeal on sectarian or class interests commands a governing majority, the lack of vision in the one party, Congress, that has had a broad, centrist outlook is of some concern. Political opportunism, feeding on widespread discontent and frustration, will only deepen the problems now facing the country. India must achieve stability through a government strong enough to stem the rise of Hindu militancy, obtain an armistice in the inter-caste wars, make peace with the separatists and so create a favorable environment for growth and investment. Failing this, government revenues will continue to shrink as disruption of production and distribution slows economic growth, as overseas investors become chary of putting their money into the country, and as rising tax rates necessitated by declining revenues inspire more than usual noncompliance with the tax laws.

At the same time, government costs will continue to escalate as additional borrowings are required to compensate for inadequate revenues, as more funds are needed for policing and armaments outlays, and as costly programs and concessions continue to be put up for disadvantaged and politically troublesome groups that in a climate of economic growth might be able to take care of themselves. For a country that lacks a strong natural resource base, such as oil, and, like India, has rejected the idea of authoritarian rule, successful economic development requires an effective multi-party democracy, safeguards for human rights and the unchallenged rule of law. On all these counts India, currently, faces problems.

The restlessness in India today stems, we have argued, from a poorly accommodated cultural diversity in an context of disappointing and unfairly distributed economic growth. The problems we have described are, in part, symptomatic of a necessary transition to new modes of organization. Such transitions are rarely smooth. In the Indian case, the emergence of a new order is hampered by pervasive mistrust of the very agencies and institutions which, under the prevailing polity, are looked to for new solutions. Corruption, malfeasance, bureaucratic delays and inaction—the grist of gossip, crusading journalism and an unending string of inquiring commissions and committees—breed deep cynicism in a population that has seldom experienced the benefits of a relatively enlightened and effective government committed to social betterment. It is not surprising therefore that loyalties and allegiances remain narrowly defined, confined to the circles that can be trusted and in which one's word is heard and honored. The consequent stand-off between rulers and ruled affects all aspects of extra-familial life, from reluctance to cooperate with authority, to skepticism toward official programs and the officials who run them. An underdeveloped devotion to the common weal and purpose is not unique to India. It is character-istic of societies in which family and village based institutions are outgrown before their replacements are fully formed and accepted.

Much of the day-to-day functioning of the Indian government at all levels, is taken up with treating the symptoms of social change as these are manifest in social conflict and the competing, often clamorous, claims of the "dominant propertied classes" (Bardhan) and those who aspire to join their ranks. Attempts to get beyond the symptoms to the causes of social discord and to identify the basic problems facing the country, reveal a fair degree of agreement on what these are. In addition to the tendencies toward regional and ethnic devolution and the un-availing search for a workable form of pluralistic accommodation, three items make most lists. Environmental degradation is one of these, the specifics of which are familiar: deforestation, watershed destruction, atmospheric and ground water pollution, loss of agricultural land through waterlogging and salinization and the inadequacy of government policies and programs intended to deal with these problems.

On most lists also is the failure of economic growth to make serious headway against poverty and unemployment. The capacity of the government to administer effective programs is limited, inter alia, by sluggish performance in both the agricultural and industrial sectors. Agriculture is characterized, in Mellor's phrase (Mellor, 1976), by "growth without development," meaning that the much heralded growth in output of agricultural products, primarily in food grains, has not been matched by rising average levels of living. According to official estimates of production (Mellor, 1988, Table 3.1), food grain output has risen from around 55 to 60 million metric tons in the early 1950s to around 150 million tons or so today. This is a solid achievement al-though it falls somewhat short of what would have been expected on the basis of some of the inputs (fertilizer, irrigation and labor) that were employed. The rise in food production has been sufficient to permit some increase on a per capita basis, but the policy of reducing food imports—India was a net exporter of food grains 1979 thru 1981—and accumulating large public stocks of grain has meant that "there has not been an increase in per capita food grain availability in India in the last three decades" (Mellor, op cit).

Even though India's desire to cut imports and effective lobbying by farmer's organizations to maintain grain reserves at excessive levels has prevented a rise in per capita availability, the real problem has been demand. The increase in GNP per capita over the past twenty five year or so, has not been accompanied by an increase in the real wages of agricultural laborers and other unskilled workers. Population growth in rural areas has reduced the size of peasant land holdings and thus squeezed labor out of proprietary agriculture into farm labor. Making matters worse is the fact that an increasing proportion of farm laborers work as casual laborers. From 1972–73 to 1982–83 rural wage labor increased in relation to the size of the rural work force in every state except Maharashtra. In addition, casual wage laborers, generally the poorest paid members of the rural work force, increased relative to wage laborers in all states over the same time period (Vaidyanathan, 1988, Table 4.3). For many families in rural India, the triumphant achievements of the Green Revolution could not be translated into improved dietary intake and thus measures of poverty based on caloric intake or expenditures on calories show little improvement. If there was any improvement at all in average nutritional intake from the early 1950s to the present, it would have had to result from greater consumption of energy foods since the average Indian diet seems to have deteriorated in terms of protein intake (Evenson, 1986). A review of the situation in the mid-1980s holds out the prospect for somewhat better times ahead:

> We find that average consumption of all goods and of all foods declined in the 1950s and 1960s, but that this decline was arrested in the 1970s and early 1980s. For the poorest in both rural and urban India, the 1960s were the most difficult years as nutrition intake declined and poverty rose. The 1970s and early 1980s were years of some possible improvement in the welfare of the poorest in India. (Evenson, 1986).

If the employment picture improves thus permitting the poorer members of society to consume a more adequate diet, the question will turn again to the outlook for further increases in food production or the prospects for food imports. Projected per capita food grain production over the next twenty years continues the same path it has followed since World War II, even with a threefold increase in the use of chemical fertilizers (Seckler and Sampath, Table A.1). Prospects for increased per capita output of other essential food products appear more problematic. An optimal policy to raise the level of agricultural output would entail rising food prices and thus, if average welfare is not to suffer, would require the rate of economic growth and employment both to be greatly accelerated. Given the needs of Indian agriculture for investment in infrastructure, especially for electrification and tube wells, for greater imports of fertilizer and of certain food stocks, for research and for an expansion of modern practices into eastern ecological zones, increased food prices will have to be met out of real growth and not merely neutralized through subsidies, which in any case the country cannot afford.

Growth in the nonagricultural sector is hampered by excessive regulation, protection of "sick" industries, rising capital costs per unit of output, and by a tendency toward wasteful, ill planned and ill timed expenditures. According to one insightful student of the Indian economy, the impressive mobilization of investment resources through taxation (largely indirect) and the vast transfer of household savings to nationalized financial institutions, "have been frittered away in current expenditures leaving not enough . . . to finance [the] massive investment programs . . . needed to boost the rate of economic growth above its current low level, long run equilibrium" (Bardhan, p.61). The situation is particularly serious with respect to export industries. Given India's negativism toward trade imbalances (stemming from a deeper fear of inflation induced destabilization) together with the decline in concessional foreign financial assistance, the adequacy of foreign exchange reserves for necessary imports is a constant problem.

Indian economic policy is impaled on the horns of a dilemma. On one are various concessions to special interests e.g. agricultural price supports, subsidized food prices for urban consumers, subsidized prices for agricultural inputs (fertilizer, water, power, diesel fuel), subsidized credit, underpricing of government produced goods and services, giveaway subsidies for exporters, tax exemptions for farmers, plus a great variety of schemes and projects designed to absorb the unemployed into the wage earning population. Leaving aside losses from government owned operations and services and ignoring the waste due to overmanning in public establishments, the funds going for direct subsidies of all kinds doubled in the decade of the 1950s, nearly quadrupled during the next ten years and increased more than 10 fold between 1970–71 and 1980–81 (Bardhan, p.62). These policies have produced an enormous drain on potential investment funds and are a major reason for India's inferior competitive position in world markets. The steep, steady rise in capital output ratios, which act to attenuate the development impact of such funds as are available for investment, has a technical component to be sure but, as Bardhan notes, the trend also reflects a rising tide of "patronage, favoritism, plunder and pilferage, ill conceived-politically prompted projects, overstaffing, featherbedding, cronyism, gross mismanagement and inefficiency" (Bardhan p.68). On the other horn of the dilemma is the government's policy with respect to economic expansion. To stimulate economic growth through monetary policies could, through its inflationary impact on a population with a dangerously low per capita income, undermine the legitimacy of the "dominant classes."

Population Growth and the National Agenda

On top of the problems we have described, India has been faced with a relentless growth of population in a physical environment that has become ever more inelastic. The negative consequences of rapid population growth have long been recognized by Indian leaders. A skeptic might even be tempted to conclude that population growth has been seized upon as a convenient scapegoat for the failure of successive Indian governments to deliver on their promises to eradicate poverty and for the alarming degradation of the environment which has been permitted to occur. But many Indian leaders are no doubt sincere when they state that population growth is the country's "number one problem."

There can be no doubt that rapid population growth belongs as a priority item on the national agenda. Almost any goal of national policy—increased literacy and education, improved health and sanitation, provision of energy and other basic resources, poverty eradication, housing and urban rehabilitation, food subsidization, credit extension, job creation, investment in infrastructure, protection of the environment—would be within closer reach if the nation's energies and resources were less consumed in maintaining the current population and providing for its future growth. According to one set of estimates (Goryacheva, Table 3), "demographic investment," i.e. the investment required to maintain additional population at an undiminished level of living, takes a large and increasing share of the increase in national income. In a time series running from 1951–52 through 1978–79, "demographic investment" exceeded the growth of national income in 16 out of 24 years. Even in the most favorable years, "demographic investment" amounted to half or more of the increase in national income. Thus funds diverted from development to take care of population growth have been a substantial though generally unrecognized item in the national accounts.-

The problem for the economy is not simply one of population increase. Over the period covered by Goryacheva'a observations, a fairly steady rise in the capital requirements for the production of income—a result of growing capital intensity in some sectors of production and, as noted earlier, widespread inefficiency in the organization of production—adds to the investment needed to stay even.

Population growth figures in India's future in more subtle and indirect ways also. The social ferment that is evident throughout India is not a direct or simple expression of population pressure but population growth and the consequent increase in competition for land and status are at the root of fundamental social changes that are transforming Indian society. In a virtuoso deductive analysis of the effects of increasing population density, Binswanger and McIntire (1987) indicate how the requirement for increased land productivity resulting from population growth leads to changes in agricultural practises, to shifts in technology, to investment in infrastructure, to various forms of labor specialization, to a change from general to specific land rights, to a reduction in the availability of common property resources, to changes in credit mechanisms and ways of dealing with risk. Each of these changes has further ramifications, for example the emergence of a market in land encourages the separation of land from lineage and raises the possibility of land alienation. It also provides the conditions for the appearance of a new class of money lenders and lending practises based on the use of land as a new and superior form of collateral. Ultimately these changes bring about an elaboration of the occupational structure, and a revision of status systems within local communities. If the increase in population density is accompanied by innovations in technology, e.g. new sources of draft power, and if there is a lessening of community isolation, as for example with the building of roads or through trade in specialized crops, the effects, according to Binswanger and McIntyre, will be amplified further.

Tears in the Social Fabric

Unlike some agrarian societies that have undergone fundamental social and economic change in the transition from land abundance to relative land scarcity, India has, until recently, witnessed few peasant revolts serious enough to have posed a threat to the state (Bouton,1985). But there appears to be widespread and growing challenge to traditional hierarchical relationships and, in particular, to the relationship between landlord and peasant. As Binswanger and McIntire point out, the patron-client relationship itself is an emergent result of the shift from land abundance to land scarcity. That shift produced a class of landless farmers who could neither buy back the land they had lost nor depend on their lineage for a livelihood. Under such conditions dependence on a patron became a strategy for survival. That system is increasingly threatened as the "moral economy" of the idealized Indian village is drawn ever more intimately into symbiotic contact with the larger society.

There is still enough resilience and absorptive capacity in the Indian village to prevent mass exodus to the cities (Das Gupta, 1987) but traditional rights and obligations are under increasing pressure. To take an everyday example, the poor can no longer count on free distribution of the buttermilk left after the landlord uses what milk he needs to make butter. In the absence of a developed market for milk, the landlord had no better way of disposing of surplus buttermilk. Now, however, with the organization of direct distribution of milk to urban consumers through collection and marketing mechanisms pioneered by the National Dairy Development Board and other farmers groups. the local distribution of free, surplus milk products has virtually disappeared. In similar vein, it has been pointed out by Das Gupta and others that before villages experienced the crowding that came with population growth, the poor enjoyed a traditional right to collect dung from streets and lanes. Now that the claimants for this "common property resource" have become more numerous, some village councils in order to prevent contentious squabbling have ruled that dung belongs to the owner of the cattle (Das Gupta,ibid). A more down to earth example of the "reduction of common property resources" and the concomitant expansion of private property rights can hardly be imagined. These homely illustrations are the mere brush strokes of the larger picture painted by observers like Das Gupta who writes:

> The direct sources of income based on hereditary service relationships have become largely defunct because they have ceased to be valuable for the landowner. The major factors behind this process are the commercialization of agriculture, population pressure on the land, and technological changes replacing artisan work and some other forms of labor. Because of highly unequal power, reflected in the ownership of land and in the caste system, the poor are in no position to effectively enforce their traditional rights. The breakdown of this traditional village socio-economic organization and its accompanying tensions have been documented in village studies from all over the country. (Das Gupta, ibid).

The social and political consequences of population growth, while evident in post hoc interpretations, are subject to few safe generalizations. In some demographic-ecological settings, for example the Central Java described by Geertz (Geertz,1963), population growth can be absorbed through an elaboration and modification of economic, technological and cultural practises without direct challenge to traditional hierarchical relationships. In central Java this meant the sharing of poverty and accepting a fall in labor productivity. Under other conditions, for example as in Czarist Russia or pre-Communist China, where, perhaps because social organization was less resilient and disparities in opportunity more flagrant and visible than in the Central Java, revolt was endemic, needing only the periodic emergence of revolutionary leadership.

The segmented, hierarchical, nature of Indian society is like neither of these. It is neither as absorptive and accommodative as Geertz' Java nor as prone to revolutionary upheaval as Russia or China. In India unrest tends to be channeled into localized movements that aim to enhance the groups position *within the system*. Which is not to say that serious outbreaks of violence will not occur on other grounds, as in the case of communal strife between Muslims and Hindus or the demands for autonomy by Sikh nationalists. Otherwise, and with few exceptions, such as the 1948 peasant uprising in Hyderabad, India has experienced more maneuver and manipulation than revolutionary outbreak in the search for social advantage. The recent protest by farmers in Meerut in western Uttar Pradesh, which has been described as "unprecedented" and as "an exhibition of people's power at its most impressive" (*India Today*, Feb. 29, 1988), is essentially a demand for the redress *by the authorities* of certain perceived inequities. While this protest has been disconcerting politically and while meeting the farmer's demands will be painful for the government, there is no direct or implied challenge to the system as such. It is, in essence, an appeal to authority and has been dealt with as such—as a clamorous demand to be handled by measures such as cutting the cost of fertilizer, reducing interest rates on agricultural loans, tax concessions and increased spending on the agricultural sector (*The Economist*, 11 March, 1988). Interesting also are the demands themselves. In addition to short term economic relief from the effects of the most devastating drought of the century, the farmer's demanded that government jobs be "reserved" for their children and that funds be established to provide pensions for farmers. Thus while the Meerut *dharna* reflected revolutionary changes that are occurring in Indian society, it was not itself, at this point at least, revolutionary in its aims.

The containment of protest is evidence of the persistence of what has been called clientelism in Indian rural society. Despite the acknowledged failure of land reform (since the expropriation of the zamindars), despite the increase in landlessness and the decline in real terms in farm wages (Bardhan, p 190), and despite too, the chronically ineffective nature of government programs to reduce and alleviate poverty (Kohli, 1989), the poor in India remain too dependent on the system to attack it head-on.

Organized protest is difficult to sustain at an effective level in the context of the dependency relationships between landlord, tenant and agricultural laborer. As ring masters of the local economy, landlords are able through the bestowing of tenancy agreements and labor contracts to maintain the system of dependency and thus to undermine any tendency toward coalescence among aggrieved classes. In an analysis of agrarian class formation, Bardhan concludes that:

> . . .personalized clientelization fragments the labor market, fractures the formation of class consciousness, and emasculates class organization . . . such clientelization largely arises from the absence of credit and insurance markets. . . . In the cases in which class action taken by poor peasants and laborers fails, the consequences in terms of exposure to insecurities and oppression are sometimes much worse than the status quo ante. It is the high risk of failure and the deep doubts of organizational feasibility and sustainability of class action that get internalized in the peasant mind, and their behavioral expressions take forms that are often interpreted as quiescence or false consciousness. (Bardhan, op cit. p 187)

There is little question, however, that the terms of the relationships among lord and peasant and between traditional occupational groups are changing with far reaching implications for the future character of Indian society. Even in Bardhan's view, the "social and political flux" in India today, makes it likely that the "submergence of class tensions cannot remain deep for long, and all kinds of latent structural conflicts have started coming out into the open with increasing regularity" (Bardhan, ibid). Population growth gets involved in this process by inducing greater competition for land and by encouraging other structural changes in agriculture. Eventually this leads to a redistribution of population into situations in which old skills and habits become irrelevant. This gives point to literacy and to formal education and justifies investment in, what Western theorists like to call, "child quality," a large component of which is education. Thus demographic change brings about the conditions that produce further demographic and social change. The process rarely proceeds smoothly but the forces it generates, though virtually irresistible, need not provoke violence. If the changes unfold gradually and if acceptable niches are provided in the new division of labor for those whose lines of activity are being closed out or curtailed, there can be an orderly advance to a more complex level of organization.

In the long run, India's problem of population and its problems of development are solvable. Left alone, many will solve themselves. Yet there are avoidable costs, dislocations and breakdowns in social functioning that a wise, well administered society should try to prevent. As much as by its rate of population growth, India's course of future development and the integrity of its social organization will be determined by its capacity to formulate and implement sound policy, including an effective policy to moderate the rate of population growth. However, among those who hold political power and among those who seek to be their replacements, numbers (i.e. constituents and supporters) are the coin of the political realm. The same is true among groups in Indian society engaged in jockeying and jousting for privilege and recognition. Here too, numbers count. Thus, while slowing the rate of population growth receives general rhetorical endorsement as part of the national agenda, it commands little attention in the arenas of political and social struggle.

2

India's Population Growth in Historical Perspective

The Dim Past

India has long been a populous society. Invading armies under Alexander several centuries before the beginning of the Christian era encountered mass formations, estimated by Pliny, admittedly several centuries later, at 700,000 men. By the mobilization ratios obtaining at that time, a field force of such size implied a very substantial population base. That was Northern India. Also in that ancient period, there were impressive kingdoms in South India. Estimates of the overall population of ancient India have been compounded from archaeological evidence and from historical and literary materials. At best they can be taken only as "conjectural approximations" (Nath, cited in UN, 1982). The sylvan settings of many ancient stories and legends together with the seemingly contradictory reports of foreign visitors commenting on the large number of inhabitants (UN, op cit), suggest that the 100 to 140 million inhabitants estimated by Nath must have lived in relatively dense concentrations around centers of power served by rural hinterlands cut into the surrounding forest. As there are today, there would also have been tribal populations living in the forests as hunters, gatherers and as primitive agriculturalists.

From such evidence as can be assembled, there appears to have been little cumulative growth of population up to the coming of the Moguls. Estimates by various scholars for A.D. 1600 all fall within the range estimated by Nath for 300 B.C.(UN, op cit). A.D. 1600 falls near the end of the life of the great emperor Akbar, whose reign paralleled that of Elizabeth of England. Under Akbar Mogul rule was extended throughout all but the southern tip of India.

Over the next 200 years, i.e. up to 1800, periods of growth alternated with periods of catastrophe and decline brought on, typically, by famine and pestilence. If one accepts the estimate for 1800 made by Davis (Davis, 1951), India began the 19th Century with no more people, perhaps even less, than it had at the end of Akbar's reign. Davis, however, acknowledges the likelihood of underestimation in his estimates, and in those of others, because of the tendency to slight the population of rural areas. Later estimates by the Indian Statistical Institute, Calcutta, (Mahalanobis and Bhattacharya,1976) put the figure for 1800 at a substantially higher level which, if they are correct, implies an average annual growth rate between 1600 and 1800 of 0.33 percent. This is probably closer to what actually happened over this two hundred year period than Davis' conclusion of no net growth. In another sense, however, any average rate of growth calculated for this period is relatively meaningless as a characterization of the reality experienced by the population. Davis is undoubtedly correct in his depiction of wide oscillations of periods of growth and decline. It is likely, nevertheless, that at some point during the 18th Century India began a course of irregular but slow, cumulative growth.

Terra (Relatively) Firma

The first Indian Census was conducted in 1881. It counted a population of 254 million within the borders of that day. Over 80 percent of that number (211 million) lived in the area of present day India. Accepting these numbers as the best available, the growth of population from 1800 up to the time of the 1881 Census appears to have continued at about its previous rate. Modest, irregular growth continued until after World War I (Table 2.1). Since then the growth rate has tended upward, reaching and surpassing 2 percent per annum in the years since Independence.

It is unlikely that the rate of population growth will drop much below 2 percent during the remainder of this century although with fertility finally having started to fall, some slight dampening of the rate can be expected. A population in excess of one billion before the end of the century is, therefore, a virtual certainty (Table 2.1). With a reasonable adjustment for undercounting of the Census base population used in these projections, the projected figure for the year 2001 would exceed that shown in Table 2.1 by an additional 30 million or so.

Thus after centuries of relative demographic quiescence, India's population began to grow slowly in the latter part of the 18th century and throughout the 19th. It entered a period of accelerated growth after

TABLE 2.1   Population and Vital Rates, India, 1881–2001

Year	Population (millions)	Annual Growth Rate	CBR	CDR
1881	210.9	0.9	—	—
1891	231.4	0.8	48.9	41.3
1901	238.4	0.3	45.8	44.4
1911	252.1	0.6	49.2	42.6
1921	251.3	-0.0	48.1	47.2
1931	279.0	1.0	46.4	36.3
1941	318.7	1.3	45.2	31.2
1951	361.1	1.3	39.9	27.4
1961	439.2	2.0	41.7	22.8
1971	547.8	2.2	41.2	19.0
1981	685.2	2.2	37.2	14.8
1986	774.8	2.3	35.0	11.8
1991	843.9	2.3	34.2	11.5
2001	1068.2	2.0	28.1	9.1

Sources: Population totals 1881 to 1941 from Davis (1951); for 1951 to 1979, Census reports; projections to the year 2001 use UN (1982) Medium estimates of birth and death rates. Vital rates thru 1981 obtained by reverse survival; thru 2001, from UN (1982). Figures for 1986 are SRS rates adjusted by the authors for underestimation—7.5 percent in case of the CBR and 1 percent in case of the CDR. Vital rates are averages for the decade ending with the date shown. Annual growth rates are percents; the Crude Birth and Death Rates are per 1000.

World War I as death rates went into what has proven to be a sustained decline. Growth rates can be expected to fall somewhat as the present century ends but not before the population reaches a total approximately 5 times greater than the one counted in the first Census just over 100 years ago.

The art of population projection is notoriously inexact. A generation or so ago, demographers were inclined to project the low growth rates of the inter-war years into the future and so failed to appreciate the enormous growth potential in the Indian population (Table 2.2). The UN projections published in the early sixties had more evidence to go on and so were much more realistic. At that time UN demographers assumed that fertility would decline by fifty percent over a thirty year period. The question was the timing of the onset of the decline. Early onset produced the low estimate shown in Table 2.2; late onset yielded a population just short of 1 billion by the year 2001. Since that time, projections to the year 2000 have straddled the billion mark.

The most recent set of UN projections are of interest because they

TABLE 2.2   Population of India Projected to Year 2001

Source	Year made	Population (millions)
Davis/Agarwala	1949	459–648
Das Gupta/Majumdar	1954	594–643
U.N.	1963	850–997
Zacharia/Cuca	1972	970–1107
Frejka	1972	958–1125
O.R.G.	1974	917–1034
Ragvachari	1974	831–1032
Ambannavar	1975	928–1040
Cassen/Dyson	1976	798–1087
U.N.	1977	982–1078
U.N.	1982	936–1014

Source: UN (1982). Projections which terminated at the year 2000 were extended by 1 year using growth rates internal to the projection. Figures representing the projection of constant fertility have been eliminated for projections made after 1970.

illustrate the possible impact of the Government's fertility regulation program, were it to be successful. A population of 936 million in the year 2001 is about what would result if a Net Reproduction Rate of 1 and a birth rate in the low twenties were to be achieved by 1996. This was the announced goal of Government policy at the time and implied, according to calculations that have since been challenged (Population Council, 1987, p 71), that about 60 percent of married couples would adopt the use of contraception. Recent analysis has concluded that a prevalence level around 84 percent (Population Council, op cit)—not 60 percent as Indian officials had believed—would be required to achieve a birth rate in the low twenties. In any event, the Government has revised its demographic targets and, as it has done on previous occasions, put off the date for their fulfillment, in this instance, by about 15 years. If the program reaches only 76 percent of its targets, more or less the level of program efficiency during the 1971–1981 period, there would be an additional 40 million young people on hand at the end of the century. But if the program plods along as it had been doing at the time the projection was made, i.e. increasing the percentage of contracepting couples by about 1.3 percent per year, the larger figure could be expected. These projections of future population are likely to be underestimates since the base population—the provisional, unadjusted Census count of the 1981 population—used as the starting point was almost certainly undercounted.

Adaptation to Population Growth

Population totals, by themselves, convey little about the adaptation a population makes to its environment with a given social organization and a prevailing technology. As the population of India increased in the 19th and throughout the 20th centuries, "empty" land disappeared in the middle Gangetic plain and in the silt ladened plains of Bengal and Orissa. With the disappearance of "empty" land the primary response to population growth was land subdivision. Out migration from rural to urban areas and emigration overseas until recently has not been a major adjustment mechanism in India.

The effects of population growth might have been offset by a successful program of land reform but except for the early expropriation of the zamindars, post-Independence governments have made only modest gains in this area. The situation for most of those dependent on agriculture for their livelihood has steadily worsened. Landlessness has increased, agricultural wages have declined in real terms and the gains from agricultural growth have gone largely to the already "rich" farmers with relatively little "trickle down" to others. For the country as a whole, there has been essentially no progress toward a more equitable distribution of land holdings. The 8th Round of the National Sample Survey conducted in 1953–4 indicated that 55 percent of agricultural land holding households held less than 2.5 acres. Nearly two decades later, in 1972–3, the figure was 60 percent for the same size holding (NSS, 26th Round).

The trend toward smaller holdings is of long standing. In his study of the agrarian system of Mughal India, Habib (Habib) reports that in Dinajpur District of Western U.P. in 1815, "small farms" measured 2 to 4 hectares; large holdings at the time averaged 22 hectares (Etienne, p 65). By 1950 most "small" holdings in Dinajpur ranged between 1/2 and 1 hectare ; holdings of 3 to 5 hectares were considered "large." Similar trends occurred elsewhere in India. For example, Mirpur District, in western U.P. includes about 260 cultivated hectares. In 1916 these were divided into 47 holdings or an average holding of approximately 5.5 hectares. By 1950 there were 121 holdings in the District, an average of 2.2 hectares per holding. The population of Mirpur village, the district center, tripled between 1861 and 1960 and before the century was finished, forest and fallow acreage was largely gone (Etienne, p 70ff). Less than ten percent of Mirpur families in 1963–64, when Etienne toured the area, lived in what could be described as "relative affluence." These were Jat families, the dominant agricultural caste in that part of U.P. Below the Jats were farmers with 1.5 to 2.0 hectares on average. They managed to maintain a very precarious level of living. With frugal management, they were able to make out on a diet that, while heavy on grains, did include some pulses, green vegetables, fruit, coarse sugar and milk. Together with the Jats, these families made up about half the population of Mirpur. Further down the scale were the small holders and the landless who, when they could find employment, worked for about Rupees (Rs.) 1 per day plus food. For this group, about 1/3rd of the population, survival was an unceasing struggle. The remaining twenty percent of the population of Mirpur existed largely on remittances from male family members, mostly husbands, living elsewhere (Etienne p 72).

Proceeding eastward from the relative abundance of western U.P., one encounters much more difficult circumstances in eastern U.P. and in Bihar. In Muzaffarpur District in Bihar which some 2000 years ago was at the center of the great Mauryan Empire and in the late 19th century was described as the "granary of India," conditions are extremely backward. The dominant caste, unlike the industrious Jats to the west, look down on farm work and invest minimally in land improvement. Agricultural labor is poorly paid, even by Indian standards. Small industry and trade are relatively underdeveloped, electric power is in short and undependable supply, roads are poor. Little trace of former Mauryan glory remains. The area is known for the violence by which the dominant castes, whose holdings often run to 50–100 hectares (Etienne p 74), attempt to keep sharecroppers and farm laborers in line.

Classic Malthusian interpretations do not hold up well in the Indian context. Population growth and increasing population density are undoubtedly central to the changes that are transforming the country. But, as the foregoing account is meant to demonstrate, the actual outcome depends as well on properties of the population in addition to its size, on social and economic organization and the technology by which relationships are mediated and on the degree to which the community participates in a larger, territorial, division of labor. With so many sources of variability it is impossible to be sure of the direction future developments will take. Undoubtedly there will be great regional differences in the pace and nature of change reflecting long standing differences in history as well as in human and natural resource endowments.

On his third journey in 1986 through districts of the northwest, the east and the southeast, Etienne reports instances of improvements in real income in areas where population density has continued to mount along with continued land subdivision. In one of the villages he revisited, Etienne notes that whereas in 1963 a family required 1.75 to 2.0 hectares "to live without extra activities," the same family today can "make both ends meet" with 1.0 to 1.25 hectares. The consolidation of land holdings in the area in 1965 and substantial investment in private tubewells has permitted more double cropping and has encouraged crop diversification. While it has been the wealthier farmers who have directly benefitted from these developments, the real wages of landless agricultural laborers, in cash and in kind, have increased derivatively. Nonagricultural employment has grown also, both in volume and in diversity.

But advances of this type are most commonly encountered in the northwest and in parts of the southeast. These have long been the most advanced agricultural areas. The eastern plains, by contrast, remain backward, attempting to support dense populations while contending with major water management problems—flood control in particular. With a rich natural resource endowment, the eastern plains may one day overcome the forces that have thus far kept the area in a backward condition.

The rest of India, that is the states of peninsular India, face greater odds. There a virtually unalleviable shortage of water combined with poor, eroding soils, severely limit future economic growth.

Overall the outlook in Indian agriculture is for tough going. The advanced agricultural areas will have to increase output in the face of chronic inefficiencies in the critical area of water management, political uncertainty, and lapses in good agronomic practice (Etienne reports, for example, that Punjab farmers are failing to renew their stocks of wheat seed thereby risking a regression toward declining yields). The adoption of modern agricultural practices in the eastern plains is hampered by several factors among which are an undependable supply of electric power, excessive land subdivision, an exceptionally large number of landless laborers with few opportunities outside of agriculture and a relatively unyielding, repressive, feudal culture. The Deccan peninsula, an area of dryland agriculture, would seem to have a limited future as a contributor to Indian agriculture except in raising certain specialized crops, such as groundnuts and oilseeds, that are suited to the semi-arid tropics.

The Balancing of Births and Deaths

Death and Its Transfiguration

Until recently, the dynamic factor behind the rising population growth rate has been a declining death rate. The death rate began to descend in the years following the first World War (Table 2.1). An examination of life tables reveals that prior to 1920 less than half of newborns could expect to survive until age 20 (UN, 1982, Table 108). The evident fragility of existence, the close and frequent encounters with death, quite plausibly had something to do with the tentative view of earthly chances and the persistent interest in reducing the odds of adverse outcomes through astrological reckoning and other petitionary and forefending practices common among Indians. In those times, the root causes of death—famine, epidemics of cholera, smallpox, malaria, plague, kala-azar (lit. black fever), influenza, not to mention rioting, banditry and chronic civil disorder—were beyond individual control or comprehension.

Conditions gradually improved during the twenties and thirties so that by the time of Independence slightly more than half of all children lived to the age of 20. Whether this improvement registered among the people sufficiently to alter their perceptions of life chances is questionable since survival to adulthood was still little better than a fifty-fifty proposition.

As a rule, more than half of all deaths befell children in their first year of life. Reporting from the Punjab in the 1950's, well after many of the great killer epidemics had moderated, Wyon and Gordon (1971) observed that "... one fourth to one third of live-born children died before their second birthday. Among women over 40 years old only 15 percent had been spared the personal experience of losing a child. Nearly 50 percent of women had lost three or more live-born children" (p.203). Coincidentally, as the authors point out, this was a shaky platform for the introduction of such a radically new idea as "family planning." In the face of uncertainty, people prefer to stick with accepted practises, whether it be a farmer considering the adoption of new seeds or a married couple facing decisions about the conduct of their nuptial affairs in a precarious world.

As the nation got a grip on its affairs and as campaigns against diseases such as malaria and smallpox took hold, mortality continued to fall. By 1981, nearly three out of four newborns could expect to survive to age twenty. It is instructive to look today at women living in the same area studied over thirty years earlier by Wyon and Gordon, specifically at those near the end of their childbearing years, women aged 35–39. These women had their children during the years when the Punjab enjoyed rising prosperity and falling mortality. For almost nine in ten of them, all of their children are still alive and seventy percent of these women or their husbands use contraception to prevent further pregnancies (Das Gupta, 1987).

The most rapid decline in mortality occurred roughly from the end of

World War II to the mid to late 1960s. In the first half of this stretch of twenty some years, approximately 9 years were added to life expectation at birth. During the second half another 4 to 5 years were added. Most of the gains came from enhanced survivorship in the early years of life but, generally, there were improvements at all ages.

Mortality decline during the seventies was slow and erratic (Ruzika, in Dyson & Crook, Tables 3 & 6) for reasons that are not readily evident. Malaria re-emerged as a major health problem in the seventies, reaching a peak in 1976, and in 1974 there was a significant outbreak of smallpox in some areas. Perhaps more important, the pace of development in India was disrupted during the seventies, first by the Bangladesh war with its influx of refugees and a few years later by the Emergency which, while it attacked a number of national problems with great and occasionally excessive vigor, also brought on a pervasive paralysis of normal government functioning.

Prediction of future trends in mortality is hazardous. In general, the state of knowledge about the causes of mortality decline is primitive relative to the understanding of fertility decline. Attempts to specify the variables that affect mortality (e.g., Mosley and Chen) merely indicate where to look for causal explanation but, so far, have failed to develop a theoretically closed paradigm. The identification and empirical verification of the intermediate variables and linking mechanisms, such as have brought focus and discipline to fertility research, is an unfinished task in the analysis of mortality (see Palloni,1987). Thus all that can be said with certainty about the future course of Indian mortality is that it is bound, after some time, to go lower.

By comparison with many other Asian countries, Indian mortality is high. It requires little expert knowledge to predict that as the country develops further, mortality can be expected to seek lower levels. The question is at what pace and in response to what changes.

Since the late seventies the earlier downward trend in mortality appears to have resumed. Associated with this development is an apparent change in the underlying causes of death that may herald the beginning of a transition from a pattern of mortality dominated by infectious diseases toward one in which chronic diseases become more prominent. In 1975, for example, the leading "cause" of death was "cough," a broad label standing for a variety of unspecified respiratory disorders. This had been the prevailing pattern for some years. By 1983, however, "cough" had fallen to third rank, to be replaced by "senility," an exact reversal of the former rankings of these two conditions.

The dynamics of mortality decline in India are far from clear. Improved survivorship has not been evenly spread throughout the country nor has it been uniform by social condition. A striking reflection of the complexity of the change in life chances is the continued "masculinization" of the Indian population, in the north in particular. An ample literature on the subject leaves no doubt that, in normal times, rural households in these areas allocate food and medical care in ways that favor male members. Juvenile sex ratios, i.e. the ratio of boys under ten years of age to girls of the same age, indicate a surplus of males. In 1961 there were over 1 million fewer girls than boys under ten year of age. By 1971 this difference had risen to about 2 million, a greater absolute change than would have occurred unless there had been an increase in masculinity in this age group. The 1981 Census shows the trend continuing for by then the deficit of females was around 4 million.

The major reason for the preponderance of young males is the differential mortality of male and female children combined with the tendency to limit reproduction once there is a sufficient number of sons in the family. The dependence of childhood mortality on the sex composition of older surviving sibs can be seen in data from the Punjab, one of the states where there is a strong sex bias (Table 2.3).

Girls born into families that already have one or more surviving female children have much poorer odds of survival than girls born into families without other female children. A young girl's chances of surviving in early childhood are about the same as those of a boy provided she has no sisters. Children born to older mothers are, as would be expected, at somewhat greater risk regardless of the sex composition of children in the household. More interesting is the fact that young mothers who have had previous female births, even though, theoretically, they have an opportunity to balance the sex composition of their families through subsequent reproduction, seem little more caring of their newly arrived daughters than older mothers. This is not to say that all mothers of excess female children are uncaring. All that these data show are the relatively poorer chances of childhood survival facing a female infant if she has an older sister(s).

Achieving the desired sex composition is not left entirely to post partum adjustments through differential mortality. The process extends backward to differences in birth prevention practises. Even women who have three or more living children, the number many Indian couples state as an ideal, often have little interest in shutting off reproduction if they have no living sons (Table 2.7)

Excess mortality among young females is due largely to the less favorable treatment they receive. Studies, again from the Punjab, of children who have died reveal such a pattern of sex discrimination. Less than half of deceased female children received any kind of care in the

TABLE 2.3   Deaths Under Age Five per 1000 Births* According to Sex of Older Living Sibs

	Female Birth Number of Sisters		Male Birth Number of Brothers	
Mother's Age	None	1 or more	None	1 or more
15–29	82	140	82	81
30 and above	105	146	97	101

*Birth occurring 1965 to 1984
Source: Das Gupta (1989), Table 3.

first 24 hours of the illness to which they finally succumbed. Nearly two-thirds of deceased male children received some kind of medical care (Kielman et al,1983). To put this in another perspective particularly appropriate for India, the difference in mortality by sex of the child is of the same order as the difference in mortality between upper caste Jat families and lower caste Ramdasias living in Punjab.

Sex differences in childhood mortality, at least in past years, have been most pronounced in the second year of life (Visaria, 1971 p. 71). This appears to have been due not only to differences in care but to differences in the duration of breast-feeding. Female children are nursed for a significantly shorter period than males and are thus exposed at an earlier age to the gastro-intestinal illness associated with early weaning.

It is possible that declining family size itself has played a role in sharpening sex *differences* in early survivorship. A family's ability to allocate care differentially within the household with margins of difference that are critical to survival may be greater when there are only a few children to care for than when the mother's time and other resources are spread over a large family. This would seem to be particularly true for breast-feeding. A trend toward smaller families, especially where reproduction has been curtailed through sterilization, might also encourage greater concern for the welfare of existing children, especially sons, since the option of replacing deceased children disappears when fecundity falls to zero.

The Birth Rate: Decline and (Some) Fall

Compared to the impressive overall downward course taken by the death rate, the decline of the birth rate has been glacial and delayed in its onset. An early investigation of family life carried out in the early 1950s in selected areas of Maharashtra and what was then Mysore (Dandekar, 1959), found little evidence of imminent change in fertility.

There were negligible differences in fertility by income, caste or even by the number of previous children, all of which might be taken as presumptive evidence that fertility was not then being consciously constrained. Even if differences in fertility had been found, these, as Kingsley Davis discovered (Davis, 1951), would not necessarily have been portents of change. There are differences in fertility in most populations, non-contracepting ones included, that arise from cultural differences with respect to marriage customs, age differences among spouses, sexual practises within marriage, and the care given to the fetus and the new born, all of which can produce differences in reproductive output. For example, Hindus, especially Brahmins, have traditionally observed more restrictions on sexual activity than Muslims. Reporting on three rural Bengali groups, Nag presents data collected in 1960 by anthropologist Uma Guha showing that the mean coital frequency of Muslim women exceeded that of Hindu women at every age (Nag, 1980). For an orthodox Hindu there may be as many as 100 or more days throughout the year when sex is proscribed.

Also indicative of reproductive stasis in the early post Independence period is the finding in Dandekar's study that the cumulative number of children born to women by any particular age matched the number that would have been expected by that age according to the current age schedule of fertility. For reasons familiar to demographers, such a result suggests a static condition with respect to fertility. Even so there was some use of birth control. About 30 percent of the couples in Dandekar's study were consciously using abstinence, including that prescribed by the menstrual cycle. Another half expressed a willingness to do something to regulate fertility. Nothing in these studies suggests that these were not behaviors and attitudes of long standing. While it cannot be claimed that the communities in Dandekar's study were representative of the situation throughout India at the time, they may be a fair guide to the situation that prevailed as the Indian government was beginning to take official notice of the problem of rapid population growth.

The crude birth rate (the number of births per thousand of the population) remained at traditionally high levels (45 births per thousand and higher) up to eve of World War II (Table 2.1). Estimates utilizing the results of the first two post-Independence Censuses (1951 and 1961) put the birth rate for the mid-1950s around 40 per thousand but this is probably an underestimate. For one thing, the unchanging age distributions returned by the Census of 1951 and the two preceding enumerations together with relatively unchanging growth rates for these decades strongly suggest that the birth rate remained at its earlier levels at least up to the time of Independence (see Coale and Hoover, p.54, also Coale and Demeny, 1967, Visaria, 1969, Rele, 1987). Nor does there appear to have been much change during the ten years after 1951. A case has even been made (Rele and Sinha,1970) for a birth rate of 45 for the decade 1951–61. It seems agreed that not until the decade of the 1970s was there unmistakable evidence of some downturn (Table 2.4). By the mid 1970s the birth rate had fallen to 38 per thousand and by the end of the decade, to 34 per thousand. There it remained from 1976 to 1984, as the country, stunned by the excesses of the Emergency period (1975–76), gave a wide berth to the Family Planning program. As the prevalence of contraception picked up in the mid 1980s, the birth rate resumed its decline, falling to around 32 by the end of the decade.

A birth rate has a complicated anatomy. It is determined first of all by the underlying fertility of women exposed to the risk of pregnancy, conventionally, married women or, more generically, cohabiting couples. The fertility of such women is in turn determined by such considerations as the intensity of their exposure to the risk of pregnancy (e.g. frequency of intercourse), behavior that reduces the chances of conception (e.g. use of contraception, intensive and extended breast-feeding), and the fetus' chances of survival (e.g. voluntary or involuntary abortion). The *birth rate*, an aggregate measure, is determined also by the age structure of the population. A high proportion of reproductive age women in a population favors an elevated birth rate as does a youthful distribution by age within this group.

Historically, the Indian birth rate has been undergirded by a high prevalence of marriage. The 1981 Indian Census showed over 80 percent of women aged 15–44 to be currently married. The comparable figure for the U.S. is about 60 percent. The contrast is even more striking at

TABLE 2.4   Decomposition of Changes in CBR, India, 1961–1981

Change due to (%)	1961–1971	1971–1981	1961–1981	1981–1986
Age structure*	-63.0	+26.0	-7.0	n.a.
Marital Status	-31.0	-27.0	-31.0	n.a.
Marital Fertility	-6.0	-99.0	-62.0	n.a.
Total explained	100.0	100.0	100.0	—
CBR at outset	43.4	40.1		34.9
% Point Change	-3.3	-5.2	-8.5	-1.5

*Combines change due to age structure of women 15-49 and their proportion in the population. Interaction terms ignored. Based on Srikantan and Balasubramanian, Table 3. 1981–86 from Registrar General of India, Sample Registration Bull. Vol. XXI, No. 2, Dec. 1987.

younger ages. In the U.S. around 13 percent of women aged 18–19 are married; for the broader 15–19 age group the percentage is, of course, considerably lower. The percentage of Indian women aged 15–19 who are married ranges from around 14 percent for Kerala and the Punjab—states where a high value is placed on female education—to over 60 percent in less developed states such as Bihar, Madhya Pradesh, Rajasthan and Uttar Pradesh. With such a large proportion of women in their reproductive years married, the annual output of births will be large relative to the population. While still a major prop under the birth rate, married women as a proportion of reproductive age women has been falling, a trend which can be expected to continue.

As noted earlier, the birth rate is sensitive to demographic composition, especially the relative size of the population of women in their reproductive ages and the distribution by age of women within this category. Change in the percentage of women of reproductive age has had a variable effect on the decline of the Indian birth rate. Such decline as there was during the 1960s is attributable largely to structural demographic changes, both in the proportion of reproductive age women and, to a lesser degree, to an age shift within this group. Reinforcing the decline in the birth rate was a small drop off in marriage (Table 2.4). There was little change in marital fertility.

It was not until the following decade, the decade of the seventies, that the birth rate declined significantly. Demographic shifts had no net effect on the birth rate in this period, since changes in the age distribution of married women and in marital status were almost exactly offset by an increase in the relative size of the category of women of reproductive age. The primary reason for the birth rate's decline during the 1970s was a fall in marital fertility.

The apparent decline in the birth rate since 1981, essentially since 1984, is more difficult to analyze. It appears that an increasing proportion of reproductive age women in the population continues to work against a lowering of the rate while a further downturn in marital status works in the opposite direction. According to one analysis, these changes were roughly offsetting (Chaudhry, Table 3). If we accept Chaudhry's results, it would appear that the decline in marital fertility that accounted for most of the change in the birth rate during the 1970s, stalled in the 1980s. In part this may artifactual since, while Chaudhry's estimate of the CBR for 1986 is in line with the rate for that year based on Sample Registration data, his estimate for 1981 is lower than the SRS estimate and leaves little change to be explained. The factors responsible for any change there may have been since 1981 and the extent of such change cannot be reliably known on the basis of information presently available.

Since 1976 the only sustained decline in the fertility of married women has been among those over age 25 (Table 2.5). These are the

TABLE 2.5   Age-Specific Marital Fertility Rates, India

Age Group	1961	1966	1971	1976	1981	1986
15-19	233	228	220	191	204	263
20-24	323	319	312	286	291	323
25-29	292	294	298	256	245	228
30-34	232	235	242	192	175	152
35-39	165	167	170	128	108	81
40-44	72	77	89	65	49	40
45-49	28	30	33	25	23	18

Source: Chaudhry, Table 1.

women for whom the Government's family planning program with its emphasis on sterilization is most relevant. The fertility of younger women may even have increased.

The decline in the birth rate might possibly have been more rapid had it not been for certain changes in behavior associated with the modernization of Indian society. In their study of reproductive change in the southern state of Mysore, now Karnataka, Srinivasan and his colleagues (Srinivasan et al, 1978) attribute the relatively slow decline of the birth rate in that area to a decline in the practise of abstinence after childbirth, to the greater remarriage of widows and to improved health. These changes tend to offset increases in the use of contraception which in any case in India are heavily concentrated among older women beyond the peak of their reproductive capacity. The changes observed in Karnataka are evident, in varying degree, throughout India. Along with the demographic factors noted earlier, they are one of the reasons, possibly the chief ones, for the sluggish response of the birth rate to reported increases in the proportion of couples using some form of birth control.

Another factor working against a faster decline in the birth rate is a change in the patterns of breast-feeding. Several studies (Gopalan, 1985, Basu and Sundar, 1988) provide evidence of a trend away from exclusive reliance on breast-feeding as the source of infant nutrition. In the past and to a considerable degree at present, the chief factor keeping fertility well below the upper bound set by biological potential, is prolonged and intensive breast-feeding. By one estimate, reduced breast-feeding during the 1970s offset the impact of increased use of contraception by as much as 50 percent (Bulatao, 1984). The data for an estimate of this kind are thin but the general point seems incontestable. Total abandonment of breast-feeding in favor of bottle feeding is an undesirable development both for its demographic consequences and for the well being of the child thus deprived. Supplementation of the infant diet with solid food after 4 months or so is nutritionally sound and though it may diminish the short term demographic impact of breast-feeding, it is conducive to increased child survival and thus, eventually, to lower fertility.

A further factor that may have worked against rapid decline in the birth rate is a weakening of the custom that requires a woman to terminate childbearing upon becoming a grandmother. To the extent that women are now marrying at later ages, they will, other things equal, have their first child correspondingly later, thus extending the potential reproductive span of their mothers. At present, however, this intriguing possibility is more hypothesis than demonstrated fact (for a discussion, see Rele, in Narain, 1975). Changes in patterns of residence might be relevant here also. It would seem to be a less grave affront to custom if mother and gravid daughter-in-law lived in separate households or different communities.

Abortion, an important method for family limitation in some Asian countries, seems relatively unimportant in India. In 1971 abortion was legalized in India on medical grounds which include contraceptive failure. Since that time the government has made provision for the "medical termination of pregnancy," a convenient euphemism designed to throw anti-abortionists off the track. Over half a million are reported annually. These "official" pregnancy terminations represent an unknown fraction of the total number of abortions performed annually including those by non-certified practitioners. Estimates in the range of 10 to 20 percent of total births have been reported (Cassen, p.167) but the basis for such estimates is extremely flimsy. If these estimates are even approximately realistic, they suggest, as most observers seem to believe, that abortion is not a major factor in Indian fertility.

The number of official pregnancy terminations has grown substantially since the inception of the program but the extent to which MTP procedures merely substitute for those that would otherwise have been performed by folk practitioners cannot be judged. The chief reason given for wanting an abortion by those presenting themselves for MTP is "failure of contraception" which overall accounts for half of the cases (Govt. of India, 1986–87 Family Welfare Year Book, Table 5.3). Maharashtra, which includes the Bombay metropolitan area, leads all other states by a wide margin in MTPs per unit of population. Women between the ages of 25 and 39 show the greatest propensity to use MTP (measured by the ratio of MTP to births). They have just under half of the births but two-thirds of the MTPs. One interpretation is that these are the ages of maximum reproduction when women are most apt to exceed the number of children they want to have. Women younger than this would not have reached this point and thus may be more accepting of a birth, whether or not they are glad to have it just then. Older women, if they are not already sterilized, may be selected for their lack of knowledge or resistance to interference in their reproductive lives. Other interpretations are possible. Young and older women who, for quite different reasons, want to disguise a pregnancy may seek out unofficial abortion providers and thus avoid both disclosure and capture by the government's statistical apparatus. Whatever it may be, abortion has yet to figure prominently in the regulation of Indian fertility.

The reason for this may be, as we shall see later, that the fertility of Indian women is under reasonable control relative to their reproductive goals. That is to say, the level of unwanted fertility is not exceptionally high. Abortion only becomes relevant when stated reproductive goals are about to be exceeded. And this appears to be the view Indian couples take of the matter. Well over half of the women who stated to survey interviewers that they did not want any more children, when asked what they would do if one came along unexpectedly, indicated that they would seek an abortion (ORG, 1990, Table 3.13). Among urban women this percentage exceeded 70 percent. Male respondents gave similar replies to the question. Thus abortion is not more prevalent as a method of birth control among Indian couples not because there is widespread opposition to it but because there is not a large market for it. Many women, about 42 percent of those of reproductive age (ORG, 1990, Table 3.4), have not had as many children as they want to have; among couples who have had all the children they desire, over 8 in 10 use some form of contraception (ORG, 1990, Table 8.1).

The Birth of a Notion: Contraception

The use of contraception is, under most conditions, the most obvious as well as the most important factor reducing the birth rate. Cross national studies have found the prevalence of contraceptive use to be closely associated with the birth rate (Nortman, 1985). If this association were to hold for India, a contraceptive prevalence rate (CPR) of 38–40 percent (ORG, 1990, Table 7.3) would imply a birth rate of approximately 31 per thousand, which is close to the officially published rate. Given all the statistical home cooking that goes into such estimates and the suspicions that are widely entertained about the validity of the contraceptive prevalence rate (CPR), this is a remarkable and possibly a fortuitous fit.

Comparative international experience suggests that birth rates fall 1 point for every 2 1/4 point rise in the CPR. Thus to reach the Government's proclaimed goal of a birth rate of 21, the CPR would have to increase by about 26 points above its present level or to an overall level around 63 percent. This is in line with the Government's announced goal of a CPR of 60. The question becomes whether the use of contraception in India has the same efficiency in terms of its effect on the birth rate as has been found elsewhere or whether it will take a greater or lesser effort to bring the birth rate down to the desired level. Analyses of the CBR-CPR relationship based not on international data but on the co-variation of these measures in India (Population Council, 1987) suggest, insofar as the data can be depended on, that it may require a substantially greater rise in contraceptive use in India for the same impact on the birth rate. At present the association between the CBR and the CPR indicates that the CPR must rise 5 to 6 points for every unit fall in the birth rate. Carrying this relationship forward would imply that to achieve a birth rate of 21, the officially announced goal, the CPR would have to increase by 50 or more points. This in turn would mean that, at today's level of efficiency, *almost 9 in 10* couples would have to be using some form of birth control! This is well beyond the levels achieved by the most successful programs in Asia (Ross, et al, 1988). However, the exercise does make it plain that India must find a way to increase the efficiency of contraception, most promisingly by making inroads among younger couples. It should also reconsider its methods of counting those claimed to be "effectively protected" from pregnancy. Both are steps that should be taken no matter what the current statistics seem to be saying.

There is some evidence that the task of raising the efficiency of contraceptive use, measured by the extent to which it reduces the birth rate, will get tougher as the level of use rises. For example, in relatively advanced states such as Haryana, Punjab and Maharashtra, 8 to 10 points of increase in the CPR were required for each unit of decline in the birth rate between 1975 and 1985 (Kapoor, Table 5). On the other hand, backward states such as Uttar Pradesh, Bihar and Rajasthan achieved the same unit decline in the birth rate with little more than a 1 to 2 percentage point increase in the CPR.

It is likely, though difficult to demonstrate, that differences in the quality of the data, especially the data on contraceptive use, varies greatly from state to state as does the nature of the contraceptive impact on the birth rate. In some states (Gujarat, Haryana, Orissa, Punjab, and Tamil Nadu) the birth rate has held steady in recent years even as reported contraceptive use has risen steadily. In other states (Karnataka, Rajasthan, Maharashtra) the two rates have risen together. It is not an area for confident conclusions.

Faulty though the data may be, their analysis has been an irresistible challenge to Indian demographers. According to an analysis by the Ministry of Health and Family Welfare (Kapoor, 1989), differences among the major States in the Contraceptive Prevalence Rate (all methods) for 1975 explain about 54 percent of the interstate variation in the 1976 birth rates; a comparable analysis by Srikantan and Balasubramanian concludes that less than 5 percent of the variation in the 1976 birth rate can be so explained. Both analyses agree that by 1986 the CPR (all methods) accounted for a bit less than one quarter of the interstate birth rate differences (Srikantan and Balasubramanian, Table 5; Kapoor, Table 7). The closer association found in 1976 by the MOHFW study could be due to the elimination of certain states from the analysis or to possible adjustments to the birth rate series apparently not adopted by Srikantan and Balasubramanian in their analysis. To pursue the resolution of these discrepancies further is unlikely to be a profitable exercise. The data are exceedingly thin, there being no more than 14 to 17 observations (States) in any given time period. Thus any massaging of the data, legitimate or not, is apt to produce large differences in the results. For this issue to be resolved, a greater number of observations, as for example at the District level, will be necessary and explicit allowance will have to be made for factors other than contraceptive prevalence that can and do affect the birth rate. Necessary also would be matching data on contraceptive use that are as good as modern social survey methods can produce.

There being little that can be done about demographic structure and cultural matters such as marriage and child rearing practises being hard to get at, the programmatic focus tends to fall on the fertility of married couples and their use of contraception. Up until the mid-1960s an average Indian woman would bear 5 to 6 children over the course of her reproductive life. From then on that number, the Total Fertility Rate (TFR), fell by more than one child, to around 4.5 by the mid-1980s. According to past studies, a TFR of 4.5 would be associated with a contraceptive prevalence rate among married women of 40 percent or more (Mauldin & Segal, Table 4 and Figs. 3 & 4). Before seeing how this relationship may hold for India, we should point out that the Ministry of Health statistics on contraceptive use are based on cases served by the program, so called "service statistics." As such, they do not include the use of methods not offered by the program or methods which, while offered by the program, are secured through other channels.

Judging by efforts to reconcile CPRs derived from service statistics with those from sample survey data (Khan & Prasad, ORG, 1989), a difference of several percentage points in the two measures of contraceptive use might be expected. If this were so, the CPR based on service statistics, which currently stands around 40 percent of married couples, would be consistent with a total CPR around 43. Thus the association between the TFR and the CPR in India is more or less in line with the relationship as it has been observed elsewhere in Asia.

But as we have seen in the case of the birth rate, it is hazardous to try to make too much out of these data. Either the TFR or the CPR or both could be incorrectly estimated although the former, which has received a great deal of analytic attention, does not seem to be a likely source of major error. An estimate of 4.5 children per woman is in fair agreement with straight line extrapolations from estimates that were constructed by discounting the number of children it would be possible for a healthy woman to have for the effects of marriage, breast-feeding, abortion, and contraception (Jain & Adlakha). It is consistent also with estimates based on the association of the TFR with proportionalities in the age-sex structure of the population as well as with estimates based on the relationship between cumulative fertility and mean parity—the Brass P/F Ratio Method (Rao et al). Demographers take comfort from such congruities.

Fertility as measured by the TFR varies widely among the states of India (Table 2.6) from a low in 1984 of 2.4 children in Kerala to nearly 6 children in the northern states of Uttar Pradesh, Bihar and Rajasthan. The pace of decline in the TFR has also been variable. In the period from 1972 to 1984 the TFR for Kerala declined by 45 percent, an exceptional performance by any standard. Three northern states, Gujarat, Haryana and Punjab had declines in excess of 30 percent followed by a group of middle and southern states, Maharashtra, Madhya Pradesh, Orissa and Tamil Nadu, with declines averaging around 25 percent. As anyone familiar with the Indian subcontinent would anticipate, the "Hindi belt" states of Uttar Pradesh, Bihar and Rajasthan were below average performers. Except for this latter group of Hindi belt states and two outliers, Karnataka and Andhra Pradesh, which had already achieved below average fertility by 1972, the rate of decline in the TFR was respectable in general and, in some instances, quite remarkable. In most states the total fertility of married women, the TMFR, also declined, although, as would be expected, somewhat more modestly since changes in marriage during this period had an additional negative impact on fertility. In all states except Uttar Pradesh the TFR declined more rapidly than the CBR. The reason for this is most likely to be found in an increase in the proportion of women of reproductive age due either to past declines in fertility, as in the case of Kerala, or, possibly, to net in-migration as in Punjab, Haryana, Karnataka, Gujarat and Maharashtra.

TABLE 2.6   Percent Sterilized by Number and Sex of Living Children

	Urban	Rural	Urban	Rural
	(Percent)		(N)	
Two living children				
Both sons	38	72	280	135
One son	21	30	402	186
No sons	8	4	168	55
Three living children				
All sons	74	92	144	88
Two sons	71	95	455	298
One son	51	54	284	144
No sons	5	3	57	32

Source: Adapted from Srikantan, 1989. Similar data presented in ORG, 1991, Table 7.36 show a corresponding pattern while differing somewhat in the values shown.

The How and Why of Fertility Regulation

The regulation of fertility in India has aimed largely at the termination rather than the timing of childbearing. This is implicit in the pattern of fertility change by age which, since 1971, has been most rapid among older women. It is among such women that the number of surviving children presses most clearly on the number they want to have, at least among those who, on some level of awareness, think in these terms. The family planning program itself with its emphasis on sterilization contributes to this outcome. Sterilization accounts for more than 70 percent of all contraceptive use in India. It would appear that many couples are motivated primarily by a desire to put a cap on fertility at the point at which they have all the children they want and recognize that this number could easily be exceeded if nothing is done to prevent it.

What will it take to reduce the TFR further and how might it be done? In a general sense, anything that reduces the demand for children will increase the motivation to regulate their numbers. If at the same time the potential number of children is increasing because of improvements in the health status of mothers and children and because of behavioral changes that increase vulnerability to pregnancy, the perceived risk of excess fertility is likely to increase thus reenforcing an interest in regulation.

Some analysts (Easterlin and Crimmins, 1985, Easterlin et al, 1988) have made much of this motivational double bind resulting from diminishing demand, on the one hand, and augmented potential supply, on the other. For Thailand and Taiwan, for example, they find a high degree of correlation between the excess of potential supply over the demand for children and the use of contraception (Easterlin, et al).

A similar analysis using data from India found a positive, if less impressive, association between the supply-demand gap and interstate differences in contraceptive use (Easterlin and Crimmins). It would appear that what is conducive to using contraception is not simply the number of surviving children or the number desired, even if the latter number is zero, but the extent to which couples see themselves in danger of exceeding what for them seems a desirable family size.

As numerous studies have shown, Indian couples are concerned not only with the number of surviving children but also with their sex composition. Multivariate analysis of contraception in Bihar and Rajasthan indicated that the number of living sons was the most important factor influencing "ever use," more significant even than the wife's education (Kanitkar and Murthy, 1983). The preference for sons is generally attributed to the recognized utility of adult sons as members of the household labor force, as readily mobilized reserves in the case of disputes that threaten to progress beyond the shouting stage, as wage remitting out-migrants, and as an indigenous social security system. Sons have greatest value in highly segmented labor markets, such as those of northern India. For example in Rajasthan, Bihar and U.P., over 70 percent of young couples that already had one living son wanted additional sons. By contrast this figure for all states averaged 40 percent and in southern states like Kerala and Tamil Nadu stood at 15 and 22 percent (ORG, 1990, Table 3.7a). Village and kin exogamy also increases the value of sons by virtually excluding a married daughter henceforth from her family of orientation. The exceptional strength of son preference in the north rests on both of these foundations. Women there are excluded from the labor force to a much greater extent than in the south. In the north also, distinctions drawn in the household between women related by birth and those related through marriage are much sharper and retain functional significance. Whereas in south India all women of the same household are similarly referred to, in the north the language distinguishes those who belong to the household through birth and those who entered it through marriage (Karve, 1965).

Interviews with a sample of widows in Maharashtra reveal that to some degree son preference is independent of questions of economic and material support. Sons figure in important ways having to do with the performance of lineage, religious, and various cultural obligations that are not transferable to daughters (Vlassof, 1990). To some this might suggest that it will not be easy to eliminate the bias in favor of male offspring by introducing social security schemes and pension plans—even were this possible to contemplate in India as that society now functions. The special instance of widows aside however, it does appear that in general the basis for son preference is primarily material (ORG, 1990, Table 3.10), and is changing rapidly, more rapidly in fact than change in desired family size overall (ORG, 1990 Tables 3.7 and 3.5).

The supply-demand measure of motivation developed by Easterlin and Crimmins has thus far ignored the matter of sex preference. In theory, sex of children could be incorporated into such a measure but under present data limitations that would not be easy. The persistent joint effect of number of surviving offspring and their sex composition on the decision to limit childbearing is strikingly brought out by a recent survey conducted in Maharashtra (Table 2.7).

There is much that is not clear about how such a simple measure of motivation as the one proposed by Easterlin and Crimmins works, especially how it is that a couple intuits a sense of their potential fertility. But as a common sense notion that works empirically, the supply-demand difference appears to be a useful, if crude, measure of motivation.

In the case of India in 1970, the five states with the highest levels of contraceptive use, as measured either by a sample survey carried out by the Operations Research Group or the governments service statistics, all had an excess potential supply of children over demand of approximately 1 to 1.5 children (Easterlin and Crimmins, Table 6.2). For the three states with the lowest level of contraceptive use, Rajasthan, Uttar Pradesh and Madhya Pradesh, demand exceeded estimated potential. There are some intriguing disparities in these data, for example Karnataka, with a supply-demand gap as great or greater than all but two other states, has a level of use not greatly different from Rajasthan. It may be worth noting, since cross sectional analysis cannot measure the dynamics of change, (nor does the theory deal with it) that the supply-demand gap was growing rapidly in Karnataka (Easterlin and Crimmins, Table 5.2) from a negative value in 1951 to an excess of more than one child by 1975. The subsequent increase in contraceptive use in Karnataka, according to official service statistics, was among the most rapid of all the states (see Kapoor, Table 5). With only 10 states involved in the Easterlin-Crimmins analysis and given the disparities noted, a repeat, up-to-date analysis based on more recent survey data and

TABLE 2.7   Percent Desiring Additional Children by Sex Composition of Living Offspring, 1980 and 1988

Sex Composition	1980	1988
One Child		
Daughter	90	87
Son	83	78
Two Children		
2 Daughters	75	66
One of each	44	37
2 Sons	48	31
Three Children		
3 Daughters	65	66
Son, 2 Daughters	28	28
2 Sons, 1 Daughter	11	11
3 Sons	13	13
Four or More Children		
All Daughters	59	61
1 Son, 3 Daughters	n.a.	22
2 Sons, 3 or more		
Daughters	n.a.	7
3 Sons, 1 or more		
Daughters	n.a.	10
4 or more Sons	n.a.	10

Source: ORG, 1988.

significantly more units of observation is desirable. Present analysis does, however, establish the fact that Indian couples are responding to the intensity of the motivational pressure they somehow feel. Since this pressure is certain to increase in the future as demand continues to decline, this fact is of considerable significance.

At least three additional points important to this discussion can be drawn from the work of Easterlin and Crimmins. One has been touched on already, namely that motivation as they prefer to define it is increasing. It is true that they show this only for Karnataka and its capitol city, Bangalore, but it is highly plausible to expect this to become a pervasive trend. Up until 1971, their analysis suggests that concern over the growing supply of surviving children was a more potent factor in the adoption of contraception than falling demand. As Easterlin and Crimmins observe, this is not uncommon at the outset of a transition to lower fertility when there may be considerable cultural or normative inertia that acts, initially, to restrain a downward revision of "desired family size." In addition, the notion of desired family size is, for many couples, a somewhat vague and unaccustomed idea. On the other hand, supply, as measured in these studies, is not based on a respondent's verbalization of an unfamiliar idea but, rather, on data that reflect actual experience with birth intervals, infant and child death, marital duration, sterility and fetal wastage (Easterlin and Crimmins, Table 6A.1)—all items sensitive to the changes that are occurring in the early stages of a fertility transition. It is therefore not surprising that the supply component of their measure bore a closer relationship to contraceptive use than the more nebulous, and possibly lagging, notion of the desired number of children.

A second point worth mentioning is the contention of Easterlin and Crimmins that the use of contraception in India in 1970 was at about the level one would have expected if India had been following a transitional path similar to that taken by certain other Asian countries. The estimated supply-demand gap in India in 1970, with about 28 percent of married couples using birth control (survey data), matches the experience of Taiwan ten years earlier which then had a similar gap and similar prevalence of use. Given the volume of criticism customarily aimed at the Indian family planning effort, it is reassuring to consider that, at least at one point in time, it appeared to be achieving results that were in line with estimated levels of motivation. This is not as tautological as may appear since, if external barriers to use are strong enough, motivation may count for little.

This observation bring us to a third point which is that motivation, as measured in these studies, was significantly more important in determining whether a couple would adopt contraception than features of the program such as the deployment of personnel and facilities, program expenditures or monetary inducements to encourage use (Easterlin and Crimmins, Table 6.7). This finding also could be specific to the stage of the fertility transition from which their observations were taken. An evaluation of this general question closer to the present (Jain, 1985) has concluded that contraceptive use is explained primarily by variations in infant mortality, a component of the Easterlin-Crimmins estimate of supply, rather than by program characteristics. The Indian program's emphasis on sterilization and its general failure to accommodate its clientele imposes high psychic and material costs on those who decide to regulate their fertility. The ones who follow through anyway are apt to be strongly motivated. If the family planning program can be made more accessible, physically and psychologically, more varied and generally less of an encounter tinged with fear and possible humiliation, it will open itself to couples with weaker motivation.

These are hopeful signs. Motivation can be expected to increase as demand falls and the gap with potential supply widens. As has been noted, infant and child mortality is likely to continue its downward course and thus add to the over supply of surviving children.

Raising the level of use will encounter not only opportunities but new challenges as well, one of the most important being to reduce the number of those who say they want no more children and yet are doing nothing about it. The percentage of couples who say they want no more children has remained fairly constant at around 50 percent (Khan & Prasad, 1983) while the percentage of couples using contraception has more than doubled. Thus the prime market for contraception, those who though having all the children they want are still not doing anything to protect against unwanted pregnancy, is shrinking—by one estimate by more than 50 percent since 1970 (Population Council, 1987). Moreover, many of those in this shrinking market, perhaps 40 percent or more, have no interest in birth control because the wife is regarded as too old to become pregnant (Population Council, supra). Such figures indicate that the untapped market—at the present level of motivation and with present program thresholds—is perhaps no greater than 10 percent of married couples.

Recent data leave this analysis essentially intact. The downward trend in desired family size continued during the 1980s but not at such a pace as to suggest a sharp revision of family size norms (Table 2.7). There is a suggestion that couples with two children, both of them sons, have become more inclined to call it a day. Otherwise the picture remains much as before: a readiness to settle for a relatively small number of surviving children so long as there is a son or two among them. The strong desire for sons is clearly evident in the data in Table 2.7 which show that, for any given family size, the interest in additional children is inverse to the number of living sons. As noted earlier, however, there is evidence of some weakening in the insistence on sons. To the extent that such a trend is associated with greater acceptance of females, desired family size can be expected to decline more slowly.

Contraceptive use among those not wanting more children increased only marginally in the 1980s, the big increase having occurred ten years earlier (Table 2.8). The slight difference in prevalence of use by family size no doubt masks differences in the type of contraception being used. Those with 3 or more children have reached, and in some cases may have surpassed, the ideal family size which for all Indian couples in 1988 was 3.4 children. For most such couples sterilization would have been their method of choice. Couples with fewer children would be more inclined toward temporary methods.

A closer look into the dynamics of family formation in rural India is

TABLE 2.8   Comparison of Expected and Actual Number of Children According to Reproductive Intentions

Outcome	Expected	Actual	N
Exact number desired	83	36	34
Fewer then desired	15	45	42
More than desired	2	19	18
All women	100	100	94

Adapted from Vlassoff, 1990.

afforded by a recent study of changes in fertility intentions and contraception in a Maharashtran village between 1975 and 1987 (Vlassoff, 1990). At the time of the initial survey in 1975 about two-thirds of the women in the village (excluding those already sterilized) had not yet had the number of children they wanted (ibid, Table 2). The majority of these women had a clear idea of the number of children they intended to have and it was this group that 12 years later was reinterviewed to see how they had fared. It was an exceptional group not merely in that they had set reproductive goals for themselves, but also because most of them seem to have accepted the "small family norm." Like other women in the village they hoped for two sons and a daughter but unlike the others, most (62 percent in contrast to 9 percent among other women) said that they would stop at three children whether or not they had a son. Most were confident that they would be able to carry out their intentions. However, in common with women everywhere, a good many overestimated their own (or their husband's) fecundity (Table 2.8). While some of these women still had some time left to reach the family size they had projected 12 years earlier, over half apparently had given up and had been sterilized. Among women who either had exactly fulfilled their reproductive goals or exceeded them, over 90 percent were sterilized. Interestingly, women who had more children than earlier intended, had the same number of living sons as those who had achieved exactly the family they wanted. The difference was an excess of daughters born to the former group.

Granted that Maharashtra is more advanced than many parts of India, the village studied by Vlassoff in 1975 was fairly isolated, primarily agricultural (87 percent of households) and educated only to a low standard (81 percent of women had less than four year of schooling). Like many Indian villages, it was on the threshold of changes that would reduce its isolation, transform its economic base from subsistence to cash crop farming and diversify sources of income. In these respects it might be seen as in the vanguard of the changes that are sweeping many parts of rural India. It is instructive therefore to put the recent reproductive history of this village in some perspective. At the outset, in 1975, just under 30 percent of reproductive age women had already been sterilized. This is similar to the present national percentage but was substantially ahead of the nation in 1975. Another 22 percent, as it turned out, either had the family they hoped for or had fewer children than they wanted. Thus around half of all village women either opted out of further childbearing through sterilization or were destined to have small families—around 3 living children for those who fulfilled their initial desires or less than two for those who fell short (Table 2.9). Adding to this an estimate of other women who, because of impaired reproductive capacity, would fail to achieve a family considered by the community to be ideal (3.4 children), puts the total of women for whom "excess" fertility turned out not to be a problem at around 60 percent. The remaining 40 percent, on the whole a group that at the outset appeared prepared to let nature take its course, includes some who undoubtedly will eventually take steps to check their fertility. But many will not and it is toward them that strong educational efforts should be directed and for them that the family planning program needs to be made more accessible and "user friendly."

Vlassoff's study is based on small numbers and, since it deals with a select group of women, her findings cannot be extended to the general population. It should not be dismissed on that account, however, since its import deserves serious reflection. What it suggests, along with some

TABLE 2.9 Comparison of Actual and Desired Number of Children by Reproductive Outcome

Status in 1987	Actual Living Children	Number Desired in 1975	Diff.
Had Exact Number Desired	3.18	3.18	0
Had Fewer than Desired	1.79	3.69	1.90
Had More than Desired	4.39	2.72	(1.67)
All Women	2.68	3.32	(0.64)

Source: Adapted from Vlassoff, op cit.

other data presented earlier, is that the fertility of village women is less out of control than is generally assumed. It should be possible to identify those most at risk of excess fertility and concentrate program efforts on them. Except for efforts to persuade clients of post-partum centers on the merits of contraception, the Indian program has had little focus. Beyond greater focus, the program must concern itself with generating additional demand for contraception. It can assist in this task in various ways but a significant increase in demand will depend on broad social changes, some of which, such as those affecting the mother's health, education and overall status, are amenable to policy influence.

3

The Search for Policy

The Policy Process

Analysis of the policy process in India is complicated by the multiplicity of agencies and individuals that have direct or indirect influence on it. The task is rendered additionally difficult by the confidentiality that envelops most decisions—even those that appear to be simple and innocuous. Policy analysis, moreover, is not well developed in India. The approach recommended by experts in this relatively new field (Meltzner, 1976; Barret and Fudge, 1981) is to clearly identify the problem, systematically consider alternative solutions and issues of cost-effectiveness and, finally, work out in detail an overall strategy. These are the elements of rational policy formation. To look at the course Indian family planning policy has followed in this way leaves many questions unanswered since individual preference and historical accident have played major roles in determining its content and direction.

Most analyses of government policy in India tend to be concerned, somewhat narrowly, with policy content or with particular types of program "interventions." In the case of family planning policy, a common approach has been to identify major fertility determinants such as female education and infant mortality and to recommend to the government that, in addition to strictly family planning measures, greater efforts be directed toward doing something to improve the situation in these areas (see Brown et al.).

The difficulty with such policy recommendations is that they are of little help to those who have to make policy. The problem is not that these relationships have escaped notice. Rather, the proposed "solution" is left a foundling on the policy-maker's doorstep. To continue the

49

example, female education or female literacy, either one, is not something on which much headway can be made without careful thought to male education and male literacy. In India the differences between the sexes in education reflect the ramified niceties of a time-tested social equilibrium that is difficult to modify in piecemeal fashion. The Indian Constitution makes literacy a basic right, something that is recognized as essential for strengthening democratic institutions and laying the necessary base for social and economic development. Whether it be policy for improving the effectiveness of programs in agriculture, irrigation, forestry, health, etc., the importance of education is likely to be underscored. The real question, therefore, is why, in view of the wide recognition of the critical nature of education, have attempts to raise the level of education been so half-hearted.

An even larger question is why government programs in general underperform. It is not only in family planning that program goals exceed by wide margins what is achieved. In agriculture, one of the areas of successful development, success has rested on the performance of a minority of farmers who adopted modern agricultural practises. In irrigation, only a fraction of the installed potential is utilized. In programs designed to expand the availability of credit to farm households, or to soak up unemployment or guarantee incomes at a survivable level and many others, expert observers and consultants tell the same tale. The common factor in this syndrome of underachievement is universally ascribed to the control of policy by a rigidly hierarchical, excessively centralized, non-innovative bureaucracy with a poor sense of program objectives. It is not that the Indian bureaucracy is incompetent or willfully obstructionist. Rather, as we have argued earlier, there are deeply embedded structural reasons for poor policy follow through.

To goad this system to action by identifying isolated determinants of underperformance has little chance of success. To do so may actually have the unintended effect of providing the policy makers with certified rationalizations for the failures of the programs for which they are responsible. This, in turn, may discourage experimentation with new program strategies and excuse the failure to take a more discerning look at the policies that are in place.

A case in point is the reluctance, until recently, to make oral contraception a more prominent part of the family planning program's offering of methods. The problem of low acceptance of birth control pills by Indian women is commonly attributed to the alleged inability of the average rural Indian woman to manage the necessary regimen. The reason, most frequently heard, is her lack of education. This combination neatly sidesteps the solvable problems involving unreliable distribution, poor counselling and follow-up and resistance within the medical community. To accept the policy-maker's diagnosis and urge more education for rural women lets everyone too easily off the hook and discourages a search for alternative approaches.

The Policy Setting

Policy making in India in the area of health and population also displays distinctive characteristics that are both persistent and deep rooted. Most observers would agree that among the principal hallmarks of health and population policy are a high degree of centralization, bureaucratic control and lack of significant popular participation (Panandikar, 1983). The process itself is often "cast in a judicial mould" (Giridhar et al, 1985) employing "oral and written evidence, depositions, investigatory field trips" all directed toward "verdicts" as to appropriate actions. There are few routes of appeal from the decisions that are handed down. The goal, generally, is a "consensus set" of recommendations that foreclose any further debate. The approach, in the language of policy analysts, is that of "rational choice" as seen from the perspective of government agencies. Little real attention, but rather more rhetoric, is directed to the diverse interests and views of participants or clients.

Policy analysis and discussion in India frequently proceeds on the basis of meager and often inconsistent information. To the extent that it is guided by pilot projects, models or prototypes, these may not have been studied in sufficient detail to be able to identify the factors responsible for their success (or failure). Essential elements may be lost in the process of "scaling up." Particularly vulnerable to such transmission loss is the interaction between officials, community representatives and politicians, which when sensitively orchestrated is often the main reason for the success of small scale projects—even some that could have been better designed.

Centralization

Central planning and direction in the execution of policy is a common feature of development programs in many countries. However, as the family planning programs of Indonesia and Thailand are often cited to illustrate, this need not preclude significant local involvement. The Indian family planning program, while it regularly, and perhaps somewhat ritualistically, calls for "grass roots" involvement and for a "people's movement" in support of birth control, stands as one of the most rigidly centralized programs in Asia.

As in so many other matters, strong centrism has roots in the policies of British India. Various Government of India Acts, beginning with the need to define the nature of the central authority in the wake of the Mutiny and the demise of the East India Company, have successively fixed the character of Indian federalism. As a style of governance, it is a direct descendant of the rule imposed on India by the Mughals and their colonial successors. It is a paternalistic authority that, unlike the centrally induced citizen activism of, say, China, puts few demands on its citizens other than basic compliance with provisions for raising revenue and keeping civil order. Programs to benefit the populace are seldom demanded by it but, instead, are offered up by the government for the taking. Except for the period of the Emergency when pressure was exerted on the population to submit to sterilization and to help round up others to undergo the procedure, the expected citizen's role has been one of passive, voluntary, acceptance—a defining case of Myrdal's "soft state."

India's experience since Independence has reenforced its inherited centrist tendency. The opening decades were strewn with crises which had the effect of sanctioning the exercise of central authority. First there was the chaos of Partition and its aftermath. Then came measures to weaken the Princely States and, subsequently, the reorganization of states along linguistic lines. While in the long run the latter may have serious negative consequences for national unity, the short term effect has been to emphasize the suzerainty of Delhi. Working to the same effect were other developments related to the creation of the apparatus by which the new government was to conduct its affairs. Tax commissions were set up to control the allocation of tax revenues to the states. The Reserve Bank of India, under central control, became the lender of last resort for the states and the sole dispenser of foreign exchange. The Planning Commission, with the Prime Minister as its head, became the guiding force in planning the development of the nation. In short, the nation looked to "the commanding heights" of Delhi for direction and for the mobilization of resources needed for the long march toward development.

Crises continued to crop up which only helped to further and consolidate a centralized mode of operation. Exchange crises in the 1950s, food shortages in the 50s and 60s, wars with China and with Pakistan, the oil crisis of the early 70s, several poor harvests, all called on Delhi for action. Added to this list was the shock delivered by the results of the 1961 Census which revealed an alarming rate of population growth—a much faster rate than had been expected. Events such as these called for urgent national action by central authority. Action, in these circumstances, translated as uniform, centrally directed, activity. India, of course, is not the only newly independent country to have experienced rough passages in its opening years or to have confronted a high rate of natural increase. Part of the explanation for the exceptional dominance of India's central institutions therefore must lie elsewhere. Undoubtedly important in this connection is the weakness of its institutions of local government, a condition which is not necessarily to be assumed as the obverse of strong central authority. Writing on local government in India, Hanson and Douglas have this to say:

> Independent India . . . inherited from the British a well articulated system of central administration; but it inherited very little in the shape of effective and firmly-based local government. The districts, together with the sub-districts and revenue circles . . . were administered by provincially-appointed officials, from the Collector downwards. Not until the Ripon Resolutions of 1882 was any attempt made to associate local people in the rural areas with the administrative process, through the creation of nominated District Boards, endowed with meagre financial resources for the building of roads and schools and the promotion of public health. Later, some rather half-hearted efforts to extend representation 'downwards' resulted in an uneven patchwork of sub-district boards and village councils (Hanson and Douglas, p. 181).

There was little change in this situation in the wake of Independence except to charge the states with responsibility for establishing effective local government. However, not much was accomplished in this direction as the states "were more interested in protecting their own powers from encroachment by the Union government than in divesting themselves of any portion of such powers for the benefit of untried, and probably highly inefficient, subordinate authorities" (Hanson and Douglas, p. 183).

We do not mean to suggest that the tendency toward strong central authority is simply a peculiarity of Indian history or that it is a product of a powerful bureaucracy unwilling to see its power diluted. The effective centralization of authority is a problem that all developing societies must solve in some fashion. Solutions vary but, as these things go, India has avoided some of the harsher, more repressive ways of doing it.

Policy Rustication

Through the years debate over development policy among Indian intellectuals has been lively, informed and generally sophisticated. It would be expected therefore that the form and limitations of a centrist development strategy would be recognized and roundly criticized. In the early post-Independence period "Community Development," the essence of which was the vital participation of local organs and agencies, was in high fashion among development theorists—nowhere more so than in India. Coincident with the first and second Five Year Plans (1952–61), India inaugurated a Community Development Programme which, subsequently, was linked with efforts to infuse new life into local organs of government—the panchayats.

The program reached its peak in the mid-60s when the Ministry of Community Development proudly announced that "the entire country is now covered by Community Development (CD) blocks (sub-district administrative areas that were designed as the heart of the program) and panchayat raj institutions (elected local government) in all tiers (village, block, and district) have been established in twelve states" (Jain et al, p. 39). Two years later the Ministry was abruptly downgraded to a Department attached to the Ministry of Food and Agriculture, a Ministry so "large and unwieldy" (ibid) that CD inevitably was consigned to second class status. The CD Department subsequently issued its own obituary in its annual report of that year in which it was noted that "at this juncture, redefinition of the future approaches to Community Development and panchayat raj appears necessary" (ibid). By 1972 the term "community development" was replaced by "rural development," a change which signaled the end of both the community and the panchayats as agencies for development (Jain et al, op cit, p. 44). Development was again centralized and entrusted to a collection of bureaucratically administered, "centrally sponsored" sectoral schemes, none conceived at the ground level nor accountable to the local community (ibid). The village panchayats henceforth had no assigned role in development except in the case of the newly launched Integrated Rural Development Programme (IRDP), the flagship program of the new order, in which they were made responsible for identifying local households eligible for assistance. Even this function became a seldom observed, procedural formality. Disenchantment and eclipse were the fate also of the cooperatives which had been seen as partners with the panchayats and promoted as a source of credit that would liberate the poor from dependence on traditional money lenders. Successive evaluations of the cooperative program have shown that, with some significant exceptions, cooperatives have been taken over and used by the more privileged members of rural society for their own ends.

What went wrong? In retrospect, a large part of the problem appears to have been a romantic fallacy. The designers of the Community Development approach to development had assumed, fallaciously as it turned out, that the villages, Gandhi's over-romanticized "little republics," would take over many of the tasks of development once initial momentum had been imparted to them. But Community Development never became a "people's movement." Its benefits were captured largely by local "notables" who as members of strategic committees operated, to great personal advantage, as "insiders." The program was regarded by those it was designed to help as a government program, made in Delhi, or in the state capitol. It was delivered to the people by officials from outside who, as might have been expected, the villagers viewed with the skepticism traditionally reserved for "strangers." As the program wound down and the officials left, the roads, wells, schools, reservoirs—the "inputs" that were supposed to launch the village on the path to development—fell into neglect (Hanson and Douglas, p. 186).

Panchayati Raj

Despite this disappointing failure in grass roots development, faith continues in some quarters for revival of democratic institutions that can function in such a way as to make the local community responsible for its own future. The "Panchayati Raj," a three tiered system linking the ancient and mostly defunct village panchayat to representative bodies at the development block and district levels, has a strong hold on the imagination of some politicians. Enthusiasm for the potential of these revived "village republics" has sometimes overwhelmed the skeptics, some of whom undoubtedly recall the indictment handed down some years earlier by the revered Harijan leader, Dr. Ambedkar. In a speech to the Constituent Assembly, Ambedkar held that "these village republics have been the ruination of India. . . . What is a village but a sink of localism, a den of ignorance, narrow-mindedness and communalism?" (Hanson and Douglas, p. 190). But belief that the Indian village can be resurrected as a device for popular mobilization is not dead.

While the panchayati raj system may prove itself in the future, up till now it appears that the introduction of "democratic" institutions into the culturally divided, heavily factionalized villages of India has exacerbated these divisions rather than created a base for unified action. Again citing Hanson and Douglas:

The partial removal of the heavy bureaucratic hand and the new influence acquired by democratic representatives have combined to intensify the struggle over the allocation of the various inputs that the state and central government have to offer—a struggle in which the dominant groups, both new and old, have often succeeded in giving 'democratic' sanction to the

privileges they were already enjoying before panchayati raj was introduced (Hanson and Douglas, p. 200).

Even in West Bengal, where a Marxist government made concerted
efforts to mobilize local government for an attack on rural poverty, the
results, while better than most everywhere else, were modest and
confined largely to political gains. The strongholds of local power and
privilege were not significantly penetrated and, thus, the "relations of
production" and the tenurial arrangements that stood in the way of
efforts to alleviate poverty, remained essentially intact (Kohli, 1987).

The Collector

It has never been Government policy to turn local matters over totally to the panchayats. In practise the panchayat is subject to bureaucratic authority although the fictions of democratic rule are maintained.
The result, as might be imagined, is a certain amount of ambiguity and
some awkwardness as the reality of central control confronts the fiction
of popular rule. The time honored deference to authority retains its
force in these situations. The task faced by officials in simultaneously
carrying out the policies handed down through the hierarchy and
keeping on good terms with local politicians is a difficult one. Of more
than minor importance is the fact that an official's tenure in a given
assignment is likely to be brief. Thus he (or, only rarely, she) is understandably "upward looking" in orientation, concerned to be seen by the
bureaucracy, in which he hopes to rise, as an effective executer of policy
and yet able to "get on" with representatives of the panchayati raj in his
district.

There are other problems that affect the smooth and effective execution of policy at the lower reaches of the hierarchy. The "business end"
of state authority is the district and the chief representative of central
power there is the district magistrate. As described by one student of
Indian local government:

> The district magistrate . . . is the most central figure in the district. He can,
> by right, be involved in almost all district-level activity and he himself
> controls almost all the significant committees in the district, of which he is
> invariably the chairman. Ever since Mughal times and earlier, the three
> central officers in the administration have been the Army Commander,
> the Magistrate and the Revenue Collector (Chaturvedi, p. 183).

Under the British the judicial (magisterial) and revenue (collection)
functions were combined under a single representative of the Crown—
the district magistrate.

This system is still in place but the role of the district magistrate has become more and more confused. He is often circumvented as new programs and departments seek to establish their own direct line contacts with higher authority. Thus, the traditional coordinating role of the district magistrate is increasingly challenged by the "upward looking" representatives of functional departments. The magistrate may be further handicapped in carrying out his responsibilities if, as is often the case, he is in his first significant civil service posting and thus likely to be junior in age and experience to other district officials with whom he must deal. Formerly the magistrate could compensate for youth and inexperience through superior education and social background. This is no longer so clearly the case especially as the magistrate, who tends by background and experience to be a generalist, must often pit his common sense judgement in technical matters against the views of specialists from functional departments. The policy of reserving civil service jobs for members of the disadvantaged classes could further confuse matters if policies on field postings remain as they are.

The district magistrate's relationship to the panchayats in his district, especially the district level panchayat, the Zila Parishad, is already ambiguous, as we have noted. His relationship to other district officials has also become less straightforwardly hierarchical than in the past. In his study of district administration, Chaturvedi observes that confusion, conflict and mistrust among district level officials leads to insecurity and a reluctance to build cooperative relationships. Poor lateral relationships, he finds, result in poor performance "unless strongly coordinated by a common superior authority." In the past this role fell to the magistrate. Expectably, the consequences can be unfortunate for the effective pursuit of policy:

> Over a period of time the accumulated experience of lower performance results in feelings of nonachievement and a persistent assumption that the situation cannot be improved. Each party believes that change can occur only through the efforts of a powerful third party. . . . Each party feels powerless to influence change in the others [and] . . . while they recognize the significance of collaboration and coordination, feel unable to initiate and achieve the same (Chaturvedi, pp. 118–119).

Chaturvedi's study was concerned with the decisions and actions taken by district officials under varying degrees of pressure from the threat of drought and flood but his point has broad applicability. Although he found that the willingness of officials to work cooperatively improved under the threat of environmental disaster, even then it left much to be desired. In the case of such mundane matters of administration as health and family planning one might expect even less. Since departments tend to take unilateral rather than coordinated action even in such urgent situations as flood and disaster that call for urgent cooperation, Chaturvedi concludes that "in those situations which are relatively less urgent they are more likely to act in the same manner" (Chaturvedi, p. 105).

Despite these realities, which are no secret to Indian administrators, they seem not to deter the enthusiasts for "multi-sectoral" approaches at the "grass roots" level, who seem to have given little thought to the problems of coordination and authority on the ground.

The State

Between the district and the Center stands the state. A particularly thorny matter in the design and administration of population policy in India is the nature of Center-State relationships. Unlike health, which is more of a joint venture between these two levels of government and is actually defined as a "state subject," the government's population program is fully funded by the central government. The states are free to augment the official program, as for example by increasing incentive payments or altering the nomenclature or pay scales for particular posts. But such modifications tend to be of minor importance. The states, most importantly, are not free to use central funds to make changes in policy that would take account of regional and local peculiarities. They may, if they wish and have the resources, use state funds to augment the official program. Even here, however, the latitude granted them is limited to relatively secondary matters. If, for example, a state should wish to use its own funds to appoint two deputy program directors instead of the one prescribed by the Center, the approval of the Center would be required (Panandiker, p. 87). As one state official quoted by Panandiker stated with respect to the family planning program:

> The Centre determines the kind of contraceptives to be offered, staffing patterns, extension strategies, allocation of resources and target figures. The state cannot make any changes in them even if a situation warrants some minor changes. The position of the State is "one of almost total dependency" (Panandiker, p. 165).

This situation has persisted even though the negative consequences of rigid uniformity are frequently cited as program defects that must be overcome. The Working Group on Population Policy established as far back as 1978 recommended that the large social and economic differences among the states and the very large differences in the performance of the family planning program be recognized in the design of policy, arguing that "the strategies for the realization of the demographic goals should be suitably modified and made relevant to each State" (Panandiker, p. 211). This call for a differentiated policy was issued nearly a decade later, in September 1989, by then Prime Minister Rajiv Gandhi in a speech to the International Union for the Scientific Study of Population. The idea does not fail for lack of endorsement.

The irony in all of this, as Panandiker notes, is that the states even though they have very little to say about how the family planning program is supposed to operate, nevertheless have full responsibility for its administration. But while the states would no doubt welcome greater flexibility in running their programs, it is doubtful whether they would like to be entrusted with them entirely. In Panandiker's view,

> . . . the States are unwilling to own and fund the programme of family planning. It is quite clear from the political developments over the years since independence that population control has no mass constituency. No political leader has or is likely to make a political career by espousing the cause of family planning and population control, however eminently important such a program may look. Indeed, it is generally accepted that if the Government of India were to withdraw its funding to the programme . . . the support of the State Governments to the programme will collapse (Panandiker, p. 22).

The odd bureaucrat or politician has, on occasion, derived some notoriety from promoting the cause of family planning but, in general, Panandiker's assertion stands. Very few have chosen this path to glory.

Bureaucratic Control

The question, whether the full range of a family planning program can be left to bureaucrats, has been raised by a number of critics of the Indian family planning program. The answer is not necessarily "no." Some successful family planning programs have been so organized and directed. Central bureaucracies may be better at running programs that are primarily concerned with the marshalling of discrete inputs for very specific ends within a limited time frame. But under the right conditions they have dealt successfully with problems, such as family planning, that are diffuse and long term in nature and where it is necessary to achieve widespread, sustained, popular participation. Few believe that the conditions are right for this in India. One long-time critic of the Indian program has put it in sharp rhetorical focus by holding up to ridicule the notion that bureaucrats could conceivably lead a "peoples movement" (Bose, 1989, passim). The bureaucratic style inevitably runs, Bose argues, toward "targetism," i.e. the definition and enforcement of strict performance measures, the meeting of which becomes an invitation to coercion, corruption and manipulation (ibid). Targets are, indeed, a standard feature of Indian planning in most fields. Bose further argues that bureaucrats, particularly those at the center, are readily available and susceptible to the blandishments and seductive ways of the international community of family planning experts whose program suggestions and policy prescriptions they supinely adopt. According to Bose the "colossal ignorance" of foreign experts regarding Indian society and the venality of the bureaucracy has led the Indian program to disaster.

This is a harsh opinion in which there is much that is arguable. What is important for us here, however, is that the bureaucracy is itself a favorite target, often with good justification, of highly visible and vocal critics of the way policy gets made and executed in India. The caustic criticism that Bose and others have hurled at Indian family planning policy is similar in tone and intent to the jeers and jibes of critics in other areas. The late Raj Krishna, for example, was tireless in pillaring the "babus"—government bureaucrats, responsible for planning and directing India's development. The Indian Administrative Service and the policies it puts forward are no longer immune from challenge. That the criticisms may sometimes be biased and unbalanced—and even widely recognized as such—is little comfort to the beleaguered bureaucracy which must be responsive to pressure from above for results.

The critics notwithstanding, the family planning program and development programs in general, largely remain in bureaucratic hands. The unique character of the Indian bureaucratic system has left its mark on the programs that come under its jurisdiction. Frequently commented on is the high rate of personnel turnover found throughout the Indian administrative service. Administration is assumed to be portable and generic, capable of taking hold quickly in a variety of situations. It follows, if this is accepted, that personnel may be shifted about with little harm to the programs among which they move. The all-purpose administrator, as a member of a select corps of governing elite, functions in a super-ordinate relationship to the technical members of his department, many of whom may have been around for a long time. At times this may result in a test of wills with the technical or "directorate" staff who, having seen the changing of the guard all too often, may be understandably cynical and negative toward the "new" policy line.

To make policy under these conditions is to tempt failure. Without continuity, past experience may be ignored or wrongly interpreted.

Moreover, the determination to make one's mark in what may well be a short tenure in a given position can lead to the adoption of sweeping, inadequately worked out policies and weak resistance to political pressure. And it can just as well lead to inaction, to a strategy of waiting it out, if the post is one that affords few opportunities for stardom. With respect to family planning policy, the first two factors—short institutional memory and political pressure—have contributed to sharp reversals of policy and the campaign like character of periodic thrusts and initiatives along supposedly "new" policy salients. As one observer has stated "... it seems in retrospect that ... the government seemed to declare or create failure more than circumstances demanded" (Das Gupta,1988). The reference is to the tendency toward poorly planned, hastily introduced policies which after a short, and expectably unsuccessful trial, are declared to be failures—often wrongly and for the wrong reasons. Rather than analyze the causes of failure or prevent them through careful planning, the tendency is to reject the old, embrace the new, hope for the best, and plan one's next posting.

A related feature of Indian policy making is the tendency to adopt, change or abandon a policy on the basis of meager research and analysis. In the case of health policy, the technical wing of the ministry is expected to comment on programs and policy in terms of their technical soundness. Even were the lines of communication between the technical and administrative wings to function as they should, the fact is that there may be little to communicate. The technical wing is composed largely of physicians with clinical experience in urban settings. Technical advice regarding the delivery of services to a largely rural population tends, therefore, to be based on hunch and impression. Academic research and research sponsored by the Ministry is sometimes consulted and, while often useful, is rarely adequate for testing proposed initiatives critically. Usually expert opinion is sought as well but, lacking a solid research base, it too often has the quality of horseback judgement.

Since research is ostensibly carried out for the benefit of "policy makers," it might be asked more specifically who they are in the Indian setting. Within the ranks of the bureaucracy, the elite are members of the Indian Administrative Service (IAS) cadres. They function both at the center and in the states and districts. In addition there are certain ministry officials who are expected to function in a technical, rather than administrative, capacity. Oversight on the policies developed by the administrative and technical branches of the Ministry comes from the Planning Commission in so far as "planned" expenditures are concerned. Though it has been argued (e.g. Bardhan) that the Planning Commission has lost influence since its heady days under Nehru, it still has an important voice in some areas, health and family planning among them. It represents a repository of experience and continuity that, as we have noted, is generally lacking on the administrative side of the Ministry. The creation of the Ministry of Program Implementation has probably diminished the role of the Planning Commission. It is too early to tell whether this relatively new Ministry will be able to provide the kind of informed, critically aimed guidance that neither the Planning Commission nor the "concerned ministries" have been equipped to do.

Where broad policy direction is concerned, there is also the political side to be considered. Policy is shaped and executed by the ministerial and planning bureaucracy but broad policy initiatives typically arise from the chief political appointees, the Minister or perhaps a Minister of State. These individuals are members of Parliament and, typically, belong to the party in power. As such they are answerable to the Prime Minister and the PM's Secretariat. Their chief responsibility is to articulate and defend from political attack the policies of their administration. They may also advance their own policy ideas especially when, as in the case of family planning, there are clear signals of interest from above.

Popular Participation and Family Planning

Development theorists have long argued that the centralization of political and administrative power, while necessary to some degree, can be a major obstacle to development. As we have seen, India has had an on-again-off-again flirtation with this idea in relation to broad development policy. Family planning policy has fluctuated in similar fashion— in India and elsewhere. For example, the results of the Indonesian family planning program have been credited in part to the effective mobilization of the local community. Though under strong central direction, insistent on results and at times heavy handed, the approach of the Indonesian program "was to find, develop and organize talent in villages and hamlets rather than rely on higher authority" (Warwick, 1986). "The core strategy for recruiting clients has been a combination of individual persuasion and community influence" (ibid). In addition to program personnel and officials of various kinds, the persuaders and the influencers typically consist of village heads, their wives, members of "acceptors groups," (small, informal groups of users which, in areas where the program has been in operation for some time, may number ten or more per village), and local religious leaders who have been "trained" in the family planning catechism. The program in China has similarly depended on community level pressure for securing "clients" for its family planning program.

Nothing approaching this degree of penetration of the local community is to be found in India. Some insight into what this is costing the program can be seen in an analysis of the determinants of family planning performance in the different states of India which indicates that when people are mobilized to participate in activities such as joining cooperatives or turning out to vote in Federal elections, they tend also to exhibit above average interest in family planning (Ness et al., Table 2). At best this is indirect evidence for the importance of popular participation and it does not rule out the possible effect of other factors. But it is intuitively appealing that a population that has the institutional means to give voice to its demands and put its ideas up for consideration will make greater use of the programs that come its way if they are seen to embody their concerns. Even though there is likely to be a strong selection bias working in the case of "early adopters" of any program, it is important to find ways to "get things moving."

The Indian family planning program is extremely vulnerable to the criticism that it has failed to provide for popular participation. As Panandiker has said,

> the entire family planning program is designed without providing for participation in the programme by the people or their representative institutions at the local level . . . the fundamental organizational policy is based on a bureaucratic schema. From the central family planning organization in Delhi to the urban and rural Primary Health Centres and Sub-centres, it is an exercise in one single hierarchical pattern intermediated at the State level for legal and constitutional purposes. (Panandiker, pp. 209–10).

This situation is of long standing and there is little likelihood that it will soon change. The reason for its persistence, for the tendency of the program, as Panandiker says, to "run in narrow grooves," is because the area holds little interest for politicians and is left in the care of a bureaucracy that is out of touch with the people.

> Without any built-in system of pressures, and the near absence of strong political interest in the programme, it was but inevitable that the program has been operated in a highly centralized bureaucratic form. . . . To build the programme on an institution like the bureaucracy which is so remote from the people and with its imperial past is to invite considerable trouble to the effectiveness of the programme. (Panandiker, p. 212).

Just what is meant by "popular participation" or "community participation" is not obvious. A population that joins cooperatives or turns out to vote may be one that is sufficiently interested in change that it will be receptive to something like family planning. On the other hand, such indicators of popular "mobilization" may be nothing but proxies for social change and thus there is real danger of circular reasoning in this view of things. People in Kerala, for instance, are said to demand, to insist on receiving the medical and family planning services they use. To say that they use the services because they are somehow mobilized to demand them, throws little light on matters.

"Community participation" has been strongly endorsed as a necessary part of successful family planning programs (UNFPA, 1981, UN, 1984) but the concept remains vague. Planners and managers of family planning programs have received "little specific guidance as how best to encourage community participation in their own programs and projects" (Askew, 1989). The definitions that have been offered stress such ideas as education (relative to program objectives), "empowerment," "partnership" (between provider and user), local responsibility, and the involvement of individuals and groups at the local level. How these things are to be done, how they relate to larger structures and programs, even what they mean, remains ambiguous.

In the South Asian projects reviewed by Askew (op cit) the communities' main contribution was to provide "the tactical details of how to implement the project activities in a way that is acceptable within their community. Their intimate knowledge of the local situation and wide-ranging contacts with local leaders means that they contribute greatly to improving the feasibility of planned activities." He further observes that "in all cases it is the staff member [representing the private agency sponsoring the project] who has the greatest influence over decision-making and who is responsible for most initiatives by the [local] committee." To take advantage of the "instinctive" knowledge of local residents requires strong guidance and much effort by outside professionals. Enthusiasts for the gains to be had from community participation at times seem to believe that the local community could take over the design and implementation of health and family planning activities and see that provisions are made to sustain them. The record, while it is sparse—Askew observes that "none of the community participation objectives for any of the projects has ever been evaluated"—nevertheless indicates clearly that participation by local residents tends to be limited principally to "non-decision making activities (for example, awareness raising) and to non-family planning services," the later being, generally. more enjoyable pursuits.

There is, however, a sense in which "popular participation" has important meaning in the Indian context. While somewhat exceptional, there are areas where the family planning program has successfully utilized local institutions as a way of enhancing its acceptability and improving its operating effectiveness. In their survey of selected districts in Gujarat, Panandiker and his colleagues observed that the popularly elected Panchayats actively participated in the operation of the family planning program—and to good effect. While it is unusual in many parts of India to find the Panchayats so engaged, it is important to recognize their potential. It suggests that the Indian institutions of local government and the Indian family planning program as it is designed can, under the right conditions, enter into an effective partnership. This would still be light years distant from the mobilization of the local community such as has been claimed for the Indonesian program, but it would be consonant with the Indian way of doing things. The degree of compliance (or possibly genuine acceptance) said to characterize the Indonesian program is hard to imagine in a country like India that is not only less culturally homogeneous at the village level but has had greater exposure to democratic processes.

The most important agency of local government in the districts of Gujarat studied by Panandiker and his colleagues, is the Zila Parishad—the district level panchayat. It functions in various ways to increase the resources available to the family planning program and to coordinate relevant activities both laterally among different departments of government and vertically within the panchayati raj system. Its actions are not particularly dramatic or innovative but rather insure that the program works. For example, the Zila Parishad raises funds locally to supplement the meager petrol and oil (POL) allowances given by the government to the Primary Health Centres so that, unlike the typical situation throughout India, the PHC staff can go about its business of visiting sub-centers, holding meetings with community leaders, organizing various extension activities and so on.

The funds raised by the Zila Parishad are used also to augment the incentive payments to contraceptive acceptors and to buy films to show at orientation camps and community meetings. The usual criticism of the orientation camps, which are organized to inform community leaders about the family planning program, is that they fail to move these individuals to any kind of action. However, the involvement of the Zila Parishad in one of the Gujarat districts studied by Panandiker, apparently succeeded in enlisting the interest and support of local opinion leaders (Panandiker, p. 116). The successful performance of these institutions in Gujarat was due, in part, to enlightened State policy which strengthened the hand of the Panchayat by funneling the family planning funds it received from Delhi through the Zila Parishad. The Zila Parishad was successful also in getting the cooperation of other development departments, and of lower level panchayat organizations, in putting on the annual campaigns by which acceptor targets are achieved.

Most impressive of all, by operating with clear involvement of the panchayat organization, the program was able to activate the Community Health Volunteers, (CHVs) to become significant contributors to its activities. By one estimate, one-third of the sterilization cases in this particular district were obtained by the CHVs—an exceptional performance by Indian standards. It is commonly reported from other parts of India that the CHVs make little, if any, contribution to the program. Their "jobs" are secured through patronage and, given the pittance paid to them as a stipend, the program has little effective claim on their time or loyalty. Apparently these factors can be overcome.

What this brief review of the Gujarat experience indicates is that the system can work. That it often falls short is less a problem of design than of the failure of the parts—the program and the agencies of state and local government—to work together. This is both hopeful and at the same time discouraging for, as Panandiker points out, "the Panchayats and such other elected local institutions are a matter of the political culture of a State, and if the political culture does not encourage such institutions, there is little remedial action with the family planning programme" (ibid p. 209). The mere extension of program services, regardless of the density of service outlets and posted personnel, is unlikely to be sufficient in the absence of local institutions that can fit the program to local circumstances and lead people to it.

But can the Indian village be mobilized in support of externally introduced programs in a manner similar to the Indonesian "desa" (village)? There are some fundamental differences in the two countries which raise questions about the applicability of the Indonesian model to the Indian situation. One is caste, the primary and unique principle of Indian social organization. Even though the caste system is less rigid than is often portrayed by its Brahminical interpreters, it nevertheless remains a dominant force in structuring social relations. The congruence between the ritual and secular aspects of caste is not perfect but rather than undermining the dominance of caste, the exception seems to prove the rule. If political prominence and wealth are not enough to overcome the handicaps of low caste status, this would seem to prove the overriding significance of caste membership.

A poignant illustration of this point is the revered Dr. Ambedkar, a Harijan, one of the founders of Independent India and the principal author of the Indian constitution. Dr. Ambedkar converted to Buddhism in protest over the ritual indignities he and members of his caste suffered at the hands of high caste Hindus. That was in the early post-Independence period. However caste discrimination and violence continue to be endemic in the country. Although "untouchables" no longer have to wear bells to warn of their approach and in most areas may freely walk past Hindu temples and use village wells, tension along caste lines has not abated. Under such conditions, what chance is there for popular participation at the village level? And, more particularly, with respect to family planning, is it in the interest of any caste to reduce its rate of growth? For example, village wells have been integrated by a show of numerical force by low caste villagers. More broadly, political leverage is a matter of the size of the voting block which can be traded for support on such issues as preserving "reservations" for university admission or jobs in the administrative service.

There are no obvious answers to these questions. The roots of caste go deep into the Indian past where they are entwined with prejudice based on color and ethnic differences and reinforced by scriptural injunction to avoid the spiritual pollution that comes from contact with persons who do not belong to one of the four dominant castes.

In general there is little unity among the lower castes which, through a conscious coalescence of class interests, might mount an effective challenge to the system. Each caste tends to be concerned primarily with pursuing its own interests in the struggle for advantage. The failure of Marxism to take root widely in India by appealing to supposed common class interests of exploited groups, is seen by some observers (George, 1986) as evidence of the blindness of Marxian orthodoxy to the persistent dominance of caste over class interests. The hold of caste on Indian society has not been weakened by technological change, as Marx saw happening with the coming of steam power, but merely adapted to fit the new conditions. Although Indian scholars disagree with each other and at times with themselves over the nature of the transformations in caste relations that are undoubtedly occurring, few doubt that caste will remain a durable condition of Indian social life for the foreseeable future.

But change is sweeping India in bewildering, overlapping and often contradictory varieties. There are encouraging instances of villages that have mobilized to confront long standing injustices and, through a slowly gathering sense of "empowerment," to demand that to which they are rightfully and legally entitled (Bonner, 1990). Moreover, when Indian scholars convene to talk of social change, discussion is likely to cover topics that would come up at such gatherings anywhere in the underdeveloped world: secularization and religious revivalism, westernization, modernization, nationalism, linguism, regionalism, urbanization, industrialization, education, egalitarianism, change in the family, politicization, planning and so on.

In the Indian context discussion will turn also to topics such as Sanskritisation, a concept introduced into the anthropological literature by M.N. Srinivas for the long established emulation of Brahminical ways by lower castes in a bid for elevation in the caste hierarchy, and to "de-Brahminisation," a term coined by V.K.R.V Rao for the tendency of Brahmins to abandon some of the ritualistic features of their caste while becoming, instead, "priests" in the secular realms of administration, education, science, technology and even social protest (Srinivas et al, 1977). An essential task for Indian social scientists, therefore, is to find in all this flux and ferment the openings to the community that these changes may be creating. No single model of community mobilization will work since there are major regional differences in the demographic balances of different castes, in the alignment of status with wealth and power and in the persistence of feudal relationships.

In the face of all this sociological subtlety and cultural diversity, the major motivational tool taken up by the Indian family planning program to attract new users is the payment of incentives, in cash and in kind. These are now fixed features of the program. Not everyone agrees they are a good or a proper idea in a country like India and there is very little evidence as to their effectiveness. The payment of incentives has also been a source of controversy with at least one major external donor, USAID, at one time urging the Government toward the payment of incentives of sufficient size to make a motivational difference and later, under pressure of newfound morality in Washington, arguing on the other side of the issue much to the annoyance-cum-amusement of Indian officials.

A discussion of incentives is, at bottom, a discussion of the wider subject of motivation, be it the motivation of clients to use contraception, of workers to work harder or of organizations to outperform their rivals. The Indian family planning program has long talked of motivation and has used various kinds of incentives as primary instruments for activating latent motivation in users and for eliciting greater productivity from those who provide contraceptive services.

The concept of motivation that is implied in the way this complex area is most often approached in the Indian program is exceedingly primitive relative to the subtlety and sophistication with which it is treated by social scientists. Clients are expected to "get motivation" from workers who, on their rounds, "give motivation" as they have been taught to do in their I E & C workshops and seminars. It is as if motivation were something that could be captured in a set of simplified propositions and rotely presented as part of a family planning catechism. No doubt workers and others, especially others, can persuade an undecided potential user to become an acceptor by a few well placed arguments. In that kind of situation a few rupees or a small gift might turn the trick. In that superficial sense only does the idea have some meaning, but compared to a full rendering of the concept of motivation in the cultural mosaic of India, it is as an umbrella to a house.

The motivation of Indian couples relative to family size and composition has deep social roots. It should not be expected that cash or in-kind incentives at the levels at which they have been offered will make more than a marginal difference in recruiting acceptors or in holding on to previous ones. However, there is little evidence on that score as it relates to Indian couples. It has been established that the *timing* of acceptance can be influenced by the amount of the incentive and it has been shown also that disincentives can make a difference in the short run. This was seen during the Emergency when life was made difficult for couples reluctant to become acceptors and for workers unable to meet their birth control quotas. The long term effect, however, was to set the program back several years in its ability to attract new users.

Early on in the Indian program much attention was given to "motivation." The Ford Foundation, in particular, made this a priority issue in its assistance to India for family planning. Not much came of it and attention eventually turned to putting in place a program than would soak up whatever motivation might be "out there" and hope that this would "snowball" into substantial demand. Presumably services that are more accessible, more dependable, and more considerate of the client would lower the transactional costs of contraception and thus lower the motivational barrier to use. As a general strategy this had merit but, as we have seen, the program that came into being was not a fair test of the proposition that supply can create its own demand. As commentators on the Indian program are fond of saying, with some aphoristic license, the Indian family planning program cannot be said to have failed since it hasn't been tried. A thorough consideration of the problem of motivation and how it might be dealt with operationally is a much needed but unfinished task. To date, despite much talk about motivation and the information, education and communication needed to activate it, the primary approach to increasing the demand for contraception has been through the payment of incentives. (These are discussed in more detail in an appendix). The incentive program has proceeded as if India, in sociological and cultural terms, were a featureless plain.

The Policy Apparatus

In discussing the "policy setting" in the beginning section of this chapter, we touched on the principal groups involved in making policy as well as on the constraints under which the system operates. We propose now to describe this policy apparatus in more detail and to do so in the context of its historical development and with respect to both its formal and informal aspects.

Parliament, various committees of the Parliament, the Cabinet and the Ministry of Health and Family Welfare are the major formal components of the system. The informal side is represented chiefly by the political parties, by private voluntary associations with reasonably well defined structures, operational philosophies and programs and by loose and somewhat amorphous groups, such as the Association of Parliamentarians, concerned with advocacy and consciousness raising on issues related to population growth.

The National Planning Committee of the National Indian Congress took early notice of the size of the Indian population as a basic issue in economic planning. The NPC's ties to the Congress and to Nehru guaranteed that the question of population growth and its consequences would receive official attention once India took charge of its own affairs. As a body with influence on policy in the population and health areas, the NPC was superseded by the Bhore Committee whose recommendations still form the basis for the structure of Indian health delivery system. The Bhore Committee report, published in 1946 bears strong traces of the thinking with respect to health care policy as enunciated in the Beveridge report on which the British based their National Health Service and the influential recommendations of the League of Nations Health Organization on socialized, preventive health care systems for rural populations. The Primary Health Centres, the plans for different types of paramedical personnel and the allocation of personnel and material resources to rural areas as currently prescribed in the Indian health program, can be read almost straight out of the Bhore Committee's report. The Bhore Committee had little use for volunteer workers as part of the scheme for delivering rural health services (the NPC thought them a good idea) but otherwise it is all there, foreshadowed in a remarkably durable and prescient document.

Subsequent developments brought other pieces of the policy apparatus into being. Important among these was the Cabinet Sub-Committee, a five member body set up to review program performance with the expectation that these reviews would produce recommendations for policy modifications. A Central Family Planning Council was created as a means of organizing the State Health and Family Welfare Ministers into an effective body for the transmission and implementation of national policy. In 1966, the year in which family planning efforts were rededicated to a goal of greater achievement, a separate department of family planning was established. A year later, in a move to give the health and family welfare program greater prestige and high level access, the position of Minister of Health and Family Welfare was given Cabinet rank.

Official statistics on the number of persons adopting contraception did register a significant rise at about this time resulting from the introduction of the IUD as a new program method and a spurt in sterilizations. But then the program bogged down. IUD insertions fell sharply and sterilizations did not continue their upward course. Almost ten years later, the annual intake of new contraceptors (as counted by the government in terms of "equivalent sterilizations") was not appreciably greater. Then came the Emergency and the inclusion of family planning in the Prime Minister's 20 Point Program to be "implemented on a war footing." Karan Singh, who a year or two earlier had proclaimed at the quadrennial international population meetings in Bucharest, Hungary that "development is the best contraceptive," did a volte-face as he introduced, in April 1976, a new National Population Policy containing "disincentives" for non-users and intimations of involuntary sterilization (Gulati, 1977). The States were spurred to become directly involved in implementing the new recommendations. Correspondence between the Centre and the State Governments spoke of "making family planning obligatory" and of the necessity for "harsh measures" and "coercive methods" (Govt. of India, Shah Commission of Inquiry).

Following the Emergency, the policy of the Government was to avoid open discussion of family planning (Panandiker et al, 1978) and to divert attention to its new scheme to put health workers in all of India's nearly 600,000 villages. This cooling-off period lasted several years as the program slowly regained its pre-Emergency levels. Vasectomy, the method that was chiefly abused during the Emergency, has not till this day recovered its earlier levels.

Ten years from the beginning of the Emergency, the Government was ready with a new policy on family planning which was to be known as the New Family Welfare Strategy. It consists of an inventory of performance indicators and lists the "inputs" necessary for their achievement. Many of the old weaknesses are contained here as well. The New Family Welfare Strategy remains highly centralized and prescribes what the states must do—and not do—in carrying it out. The initiatives that are proposed have the same arbitrary, ad hoc character that typified earlier policy documents. Frequent changes in Cabinet Ministers and governments has so far delayed a fair trial of the new strategy.

A New 20 Point Program announced by then Prime Minister, Rajiv Gandhi, again included family planning among its provisions. This assured periodic reviews of the performance of the program on behalf of the Prime Minister's Secretariat. In addition, the newly constituted Ministry of Program Implementation is required to monitor all aspects of the 20 Point Program on a monthly and quarterly basis with help from an Expert Committee. The main object of these reviews, in so far as family planning is concerned, is to compare figures on the acceptance of contraception with the targets assigned for various methods (Govt. of India, July 1987).

Some Parliamentary oversight of the program is exercised through the Consultative Committee of Parliament which periodically looks into administrative and financial aspects of the operations of the Ministry of Health and Family Welfare. Though hard pressed Deputy Secretaries at the Ministry work late hours when Parliament is in session to prepare the Minister for the question hour in Parliament, the questions are apt to be rhetorical and ill informed and as such represent no real challenge to the program. There is, in fact, no organized political opposition to family planning. Population control is an issue on which there is virtually total consensus. Many State legislatures have added their weight to this consensus by passing resolutions favoring full support for the government's efforts.

By and large population control is not a subject that has much currency in political debate. The political fall-out from the Emergency is still hazardous with the result that there is scarce mention of population control in party manifestoes or in political speeches. The only time it emerged as a topic for political discussion was at the outset of the Emergency when the Congress party made family planning a political objective and the Youth Congress issued its famous Five Point Program which ordered an attack on the institution of the dowry, on adult illiteracy, on bonded labor, on deforestation and on the nation's indifference to birth control. The re-election of Mrs Gandhi as Prime Minister only three years after the outbreak of totalitarian rule and the rough handling of the population in the name of population control, in northern India especially, is a clear indication that the population question quickly recedes from political salience. The demand from many sides that population be made a "people's movement" is a reminder to the political parties that they are to leave population control alone except, possibly, as low key advocates of a genuinely voluntary approach.

A prominent group that has attempted to consolidate political influence behind a non-coercive birth control program is the Indian Association of Parliamentarians on Population and Development. This organization, which crosses party lines, held its first Conference in 1981 at which time it issued its New Delhi Declaration of Parliamentarians and called for an end to "the political uncertainty that has clouded the family planning over the late 70s." At its second meeting four years later, the Association urged the Prime Minister to establish an interministerial, autonomous Population Commission that would endeavor to make family planning a responsibility of all development programs and development sectors. The Association also undertook to experiment with new approaches in a few parliamentary constituencies.

Some State legislators have also involved themselves in attempting to improve the family planning effort. So-called "Prestige Camps" for sterilization are inaugurated by these legislators who may also move from one village to the next in an attempt to stimulate interest in birth control. Critics have complained that these efforts rest entirely on the popularity and persuasion of certain elected officials and thus generate no inherent momentum. There has been no systematic attempt to link political elites of various levels in ways that might deepen the support for family planning on the local level.

These few political forays apart, population control is an indifferent matter for most politicians. It is neither opposed nor given much active support. Policy derives from the Ministry of Health and Family Welfare in interaction with other responsible agencies, the Planning Commission in particular. In view of the importance assigned to population control by various governments since Independence, it is perhaps surprising that there has not been much informed debate in political circles of the problem and the Government's proposed solutions.

Committee Raj

A universally favored device for dealing with policy and program is the formation of committees to look into problems and make appropriate recommendations. India is no exception and may even be seen as an exponent of this practise. To some degree, this reflects the relative absence of capacity within government, especially in earlier years, to do its own home work. A high turnover among Ministry officials hinders the sustained development of policy through a process of trial and experimentation. And, as we have seen, the technical advice available within government is seldom at the cutting edge of innovation or strategically situated to influence policy. Parliament, unlike legislative bodies in many other countries, is essentially a reactive body. It lacks both the staff and the investigative precedents that could enable it to develop its own positions on matters of policy. The unsurprising result of this lack of internal analytical capacity is the habitual resort to external, ad hoc, mechanisms for identifying and analyzing public issues. Free lance critics with ready made advice are seldom unavailable but to review an issue carefully and provide the policy makers with more in-depth protection against criticism for their ultimate decisions, something more is required. The appointment of a committee or a commission is a favorite device in such circumstances.

With the growth in recent years of institutes for policy analysis and for management studies and the appearance in the last twenty years or so of organizations capable of conducting sample surveys of acceptable quality, non-government resources for the development and analysis of policy have been significantly expanded. But for the first thirty years of the new nation's history, the committee mechanism was the fountainhead of health policy. In that period a succession of formally constituted committees laid down the basic outline of the present health care and health delivery systems. Out of this period, bracketed by the pioneering report of the Bhore Committee and by the Kartar Singh Committee almost three decades later, emerged the essential features of current policy—and the major issues of the continuing policy debate.

Committees are used for different purposes. Sometimes they are called on to resolve policy conflicts or to produce basic policy recommendations. At other times, they may be used to put off difficult decisions or to legitimize those already made. Committees are useful also in articulating issues so that they can be grasped by public opinion and manipulated politically. And, of course, a given committee may serve more than one of these purposes. And while it is possible to be cynical about some of the latent purposes for which committees are established, the early history of policy with respect to health and birth control can be read directly from the work of the various committees that have addressed these problems over the years.

Departments of government typically employ two basic types of committees: subject matter committees that deal with the content of programs and with the details of organization and administration specific to a particular area of policy and, a second type, administrative committees, that deal with general rules and procedures of administration, with the supply of appropriate personnel and other resources and with the horizontal and vertical linkages that are thought to be necessary to insure effective operation. With respect to family planning, a "Central Government subject," subject matter committees have always been constituted at the national level; administrative committees have been set up at both the state and national levels.

The best known and most influential subject matter committee was, undoubtedly, the Health Survey and Development Committee set up in 1946 under the Chairmanship of Sir Joseph Bhore and most often referred to as the Bhore Committee. The Bhore Committee, as mentioned earlier, produced a comprehensive set of recommendations dealing with the preventive, curative and promotive aspects of the nation's health services. It stressed the development of rural health infrastructure and established statistical norms in the form of unit to population ratios for health facilities and for various categories of manpower. Even today, points can be won or lost in health policy disputes on the basis of consistency with Bhore Committee recommendations.

In 1959, a second Health Survey and Planning Committee was constituted to review developments since the submission of the three volume Bhore Committee report which had been released some ten years earlier. This new committee found fault with the extent to which the Bhore Committee recommendations on Primary Health Centres and the extension of free medical care had been followed. It cited as main reasons for failure the familiar whipping boys: inadequate resources, facilities and manpower. It was out of this Committee, however, that the recommendation came for the "multi-purpose worker," a paramedic who was expected to combine the duties of a number of workers previously concerned solely with individual diseases. This single recommendation touched off disputes over the "integration" of "vertical" programs that raged for more than a decade and still smolder.

A few years later, in 1963, a Government of India Committee put its stamp of approval on the integration of field workers and recommended that, in addition, family planning be added to the usual diseases with which the "multi-purpose worker" would be concerned. This led to strong differences of opinion. Especially vehement in voicing its objections was the Malaria Department of the Ministry that had in place an elaborate, vertical organization built to standard international specifications. Argument over this issue led, in 1966, to the establishment of still another committee which, after noting the differences and non-compatibility between malaria and family planning services, recommended that the malaria program retain its "uni-purpose" field workers (Banarjee, 1985).

This did not settle the issue. In 1973, yet another committee, this one specifically commissioned as the Committee on Multi-purpose Workers Scheme, better known as the Kartar Singh Committee, again took up the problem. The result was a reaffirmation of the wisdom of "integration" which the Ministry then accepted as justification for going forward with implementation of the "multi-purpose worker scheme."

None of these various committees dealt directly with family planning. The concern was always with the overall structure of health services. Discussion of these issues seldom touched on alternative strategies but instead concentrated on the more narrow question of how to make best use of resources in expanding the existing system.

No committee of real significance dealing with health or family planning policy has been formed since the issuance of the Kartar Singh Committee report almost two decades ago. Administrative reforms designed to make the bureaucracy more innovative and less subject to swings in policy direction were instituted, partly in response to the work of the Administrative Reforms Commission (ARC) which in 1970 issued a 20 volume report covering everything from public grievance procedures, center-state relations, decentralization, techniques of administration to the creation of "policy cells" in each Ministry. The recommendations of the ARC have not been uniformly adopted or implemented. Indeed some states have ignored them altogether and have set up their own committees to look into state level problems of administration.

Some of these committees have been innovative and successful in seeing their recommendations put into practise. For example, the Committee on Reorganization of Maharashtra Administration was instrumental in creating the post of District Development Officer (DDO), in achieving a greater degree of decentralization in state administration and in integrating various development departments. The transfer of authority and responsibility for selected development activities to district level elected bodies, an innovation springing from the Committee's recommendations, has been credited with improving the performance of the departments involved. Earlier we reported a similar result from Gujarat where fixing responsibility on a popularly elected agency of local government while simultaneously providing it with essential resources, appeared to result in superior performance of the family planning program. While decentralization for many government officials means merely the delegation of power and authority to field officials with no transfer of power to local elected bodies (Jain et al, p. 173), there are enough instances of successful devolution to keep the idea alive.

The Planning Commission

The Planning Commission was established in 1950 with the twin objectives of leading the nation on a course of rapid and balanced economic growth and, at the same time, achieving a greater degree of "redistributive justice." The Health and Family Welfare cell in the Commission, one of a number of subject matter units into which it is divided, works with the Policy and Planning cell in the Ministry of Health and Family Welfare in the formulation of national policy. This process is assisted by the work of various Advisory Committees having responsibility for specific technical aspects of the Plan. When completed, Plans developed by the Commission are placed before the National Development Council, a body chaired by the Prime Minister and consisting of Chief Ministers and senior members of the Planning Commission. Parliament keeps itself informed on the progress of the annual Plan through a Consultative Committee of the Parliament (Maheshwari).

Throughout its relatively brief history the Planning Commission has kept the same basic objectives but has altered the strategies and stratagems by which it has pursued them. Early efforts to secure a greater measure of redistributive justice sought to do so through regulatory reforms, notably land and agrarian reform. Community Development, a major bootstrap attempt in the 1950s to create rural infrastructure and encourage income generating activity among the rural population, was abandoned in favor of more specifically aimed programs that placed less reliance on the institutions of local government.

From the Fifth Plan (1974–79) onwards, the focus of the planners has been on the alleviation of poverty. Following international development fashions, efforts have centered on a strategy of meeting the basic needs of the poor. Such twists and turns in overall policy are more easily described than explained since they have originated both from hard won experience as well as from the emergence of "personality based politics" in which policy becomes a vehicle for political ambition (Epstein, 1983).

The chronic failure of many of the Commission's plans and projects has subjected it to a steady rain of criticism. The litany of condemnation is a familiar one: overly centralized planning, insufficient lateral and vertical coordination, unrealistic gaps between prescribed goals and operational realities, inadequate information, deficient monitoring, rigid and antiquated administrative practises. The birth control programs, to which the Commission has given its imprimatur, have suffered from these defects as have programs developed for other sectors.

A major achievement of the Planning Commission, however, one that does not depend on administrative style, has been to project population growth as a matter of pressing national concern. Starting with fairly non-specific, qualitative expressions of concern in the First Plan, the practise, beginning with the Fourth Plan, was to specify demographic objectives and the program targets believed necessary for their realization—a practise followed, wherever feasible to do so, for programs in other fields.

The record of the Planning Commission's efforts to give substance and direction to the nation's family planning program is not an impressive one. Time and again it has set unrealistic goals for the program and has seldom taken effective steps to follow up on its recommendations. Its failure to insist on good planning practise has been most evident in the introduction of new technology which has been characterized by inadequate preparation and almost total neglect of follow-up. Despite much lip service to the idea, the Commission has not found an effective way to utilize the considerable potential of the private sector and it has seemed unable to conceive of and experiment with alternative approaches to a program which has repeatedly fallen short of the performance levels set for it.

Another critical area where little has been accomplished is interdepartmental coordination. This again is a much discussed ideal and one which has been effective in isolated instances but about which the Commission has done almost nothing. The Commission's emphasis, instead, has been on highly tangible objectives which, in theory, should improve program performance, e.g. more service units, more manpower, more buildings. It has followed this route even though studies have shown that such "program inputs" are of secondary importance in bringing people into the program (Easterlin et al; Ness et al).

The Commission has not been unaware of the need for evaluation of its programs. Since 1965 it has had as part of its structure a Program Evaluation Organization (PEO). This organization might have been expected to diagnose the weaknesses of the family planning program and suggest alternate approaches but, instead, has adopted a narrow definition of its responsibilities. Even so, such recommendations as have come from the three studies the PEO has conducted in the last 25 years often do not appear in the plan documents published by the Commission.

The PEO has consistently counseled decentralization and greater autonomy for peripheral organizations. The tendency, if anything has been in the opposite direction. From the beginning the PEO argued that family planning should be put in the hands of a semi-autonomous agency, free of some of the inhibiting procedures and structural impediments of Ministerial organization. This idea has never surfaced in any of the plan documents. Along the way, as would be expected, the PEO has endorsed much of the conventional wisdom of the day. Thus, many of its recommendations are in line with Commission pronouncements: more balance between rural and urban programs, greater emphasis on spacing methods for younger couples, comparable attention to medical and non-medical institutions, graded incentives, staff augmentation, more training and orientation for program personnel, greater reliance on formal and informal communication systems.

These ideas have generally been put forward in an exhortatory fashion without much in the way of step-by-step programming to facilitate their implementation. Also lacking, for the most part, has been a systematic attempt to experiment with alternatives, to reduce catch phrases and slogans to operational terms so that they can be tested in the field, to engage in that useful, if low level, line of investigation known as "operations research." Evaluation has tended to mean judging program performance in its own terms rather than in terms of the larger objectives for which it was designed—a further confirmation of Frederick Nietsche's observation that the most common of human follies is to lose sight of what one is trying to do.

4

The Family Planning Program:
Organization and Operation

The Indian family planning program is a centrally sponsored program with all expenditures borne by the centre. This being so, the centre quite naturally considers that it has the responsibility for planning, guiding, and monitoring all aspects of the program. As we noted in the last chapter, except for the occasional Chief Minister, family planning is not an activity in which most states are eager to be involved any more than they have to. The Centre defines the duties of program workers, fixes manpower norms, sets performance targets, handles logistics, allocates resources and takes on the task of monitoring and evaluating the performance of the program. For their part, the states are assigned the job of "program implementation" with, as pointed out earlier, relatively little room for modification. As it operates, the family planning program is integrated with the operations of the state health departments. Only a small fraction of the funding for state health operations comes from the Central budget; practically all funding for family planning is from this source. We now take a closer look at the financial side of the program.

Financial Allocations and Expenditures

The total amount spent on family planning in the First Plan amounted to a mere Rs.0.1 crore, which in dollars would have been around $125,000. The Plan Outlay, i.e. the amount budgeted to be spent, was many times this amount indicating a failure to spend the money available for this purpose. Funding for family planning has increased dramatically since then and expenditures have caught up with plan outlays. In absolute terms financial allocations have doubled and tripled from one Plan period to the next.

The largest increase came with the Fourth Plan (1969–1974), a plan that was developed with full awareness of the ominous food shortages a year or two earlier and of the alarming revelations of the 1961 Census relative to the rate of population growth. For the first time allocations for family planning came within range of the allocations for health, which until then had claimed a much greater share of the Central budget. For example, in the Third Plan, outlays for the health sector were put at over 4 percent of total planned outlays whereas the amount set aside for family planning was less than one tenth as large. For the Fourth Plan health allocations fell to 2.7 percent of the total while family planning was slated to receive 2.0 percent. In so far as allocations from the Central plan budget are concerned, health and family planning, by the time of the Seventh Plan, (1985–90), reached rough parity at just under two percent of projected total outlays. Part of the reason for the narrowing of the gap between health and family planning outlays is that, coincident with the change of the name of the program from "family planning" to "family welfare," programs such as maternal and child health and immunization were transferred over from the health portfolio.

In addition new programs such as the Village Health Guide Scheme and the Area Projects (projects in selected districts in which funds from foreign donors were used to insure that the health and family planning programs did not lack the resources needed to carry out regularly sanctioned activities) were also put under the family welfare budget. In 1986–87 these transferred projects accounted for nearly 40 percent of "family welfare" expenditures—23 percent for maternal and child health, 7 percent to fund the village health guides and about 9 percent for the Area Projects. Even so the budget for family planning tripled from the Sixth to the Seventh Plan. With allowance for portfolio changes, the increase was still a very respectable 93 percent.

To view the growth of funding for these programs realistically it is necessary also to look at the growth in real terms—with allowance for inflation as well as for the fact that resources were being stretched over a larger population. But even when the necessary adjustments are made the growth of the government's financial commitment to family planning remains impressive. *Per capita* expenditures on health and family welfare together increased between 1980–81 and 1984–85 by a little over 71 percent; adjusted for inflation, the increase was 62 percent (Panchamukhi). Expenditure and outlay statements tell only part of the story. The considerable sums raised and spent by local governments, by municipal corporations, by public and private sector "undertakings," by PVOs, and by private philanthropies and individuals do not appear in these statements—a fact generally ignored in many cost benefit calculations (see Satia,1983 and Juyal,1986). Not only do these calculations *include* costs, such as those for MCH or immunization, which one might not wish to include in estimating family planning expenditures, but they generally *exclude*, for lack of easily assembled data, costs such as those previously mentioned *plus* expenditures, both direct and in the form of contributed personnel time, by other government departments e.g. revenue, education, agriculture etc.

Were this not enough of a headache for the cost-effectiveness analyst, there is the problem of correctly accounting for the considerable time spent by health workers on family planning and the time family planning workers devote to health activities. About all that can be concluded is that the sums spent on family planning are far greater than government outlay and expenditure statements indicate. It is somewhat surprising that in a country whose financial resources for development are strained that those in charge of the family planning program have not undertaken to make an estimate of total expenditures in this area. Lacking a firm idea of how much is actually being spent on family planning, the periodic claims that more money is needed would appear in large part to be political in origin. Funds from foreign donors available to the family planning program at present run at around 10 percent of the centre's announced family planning expenditures. For more on foreign assistance, see Appendix B.

Program Organization

To understand how the family planning program operates it is necessary to consider the various kinds of personnel that function at different levels (see Appendix A), their duties and the problems they encounter in doing their assigned jobs. Some of those on whom the program depends are volunteers or petty practitioners of one sort or another; others are government employees. We shall begin by examining village level workers and proceed upward to the Primary Health Centre and to operations at the state level.

Village Level Volunteers: The Dai

Presently there are two types of family planning "volunteers" working in Indian villages: the trained midwife or trained "dai" and the Village Health Guide (VHG). Dais, if selected for training, receive a month of instruction in basic midwifery in which great stress is placed on sanitary procedures. After completing their training, they are supposed to be given a kit containing simple items useful at delivery and a reference manual (many do not receive them) and returned to their villages to resume their job of attending to deliveries and a broad range of "female problems."

Attempts to upgrade the skills of indigenous practitioners, the dai in particular, can be traced back to the colonial period. Subsequently, the Bhore Committee accepted the dai as an inevitable part of the rural health care system and so proceeded to prescribe a course of training for them. In so far as possible, the Committee stressed, training should be directed toward younger dais. The stereotypical dai in those days was pictured as an aging, illiterate, low status, widow with little appreciation for standards of cleanliness and with little potential for self-improvement.

Surprisingly little is known about present day dais, for example, how many there are or whether those who have been trained provide better care than those who lack such training. Dais are drawn predominantly from the lower castes and, on average, are considerably older than other health workers (Jeffery, pp.274–276). In a study of dais undergoing training in Uttar Pradesh, all were found to be illiterate, three-quarters were from scheduled castes and nearly one-quarter were widows.

The training given to dais has received harsh criticism. First of all, it varies greatly in quality. It has been alleged, for example, that the language of instruction may not be one that the dai understands so that about all that comes through is the importance of cleanliness (Narayana and Acharya). As to whether the training produces a more qualified dai, a study in Uttar Pradesh found that dais who have been trained are more likely than those who have not to urge pregnant women to be immunized against tetanus and to be treated for anemia, both serious health problems in that area. However, when it comes to such practical matters as washing their hands with soap or boiling the instrument used to cut the umbilicus, trained and untrained dais appear to be little different (Kumar et al, reported in Jeffery).

Dais are supposed to receive Rs. 2 for each unregistered delivery and, in an effort to improve the completeness of vital registration, Rs. 3 for each birth that is registered. They are entitled also to Rs. 2 for each prenatal referral to the Primary Health Centre (PHC) but such claims often go unpaid for long periods (David and Narayana,1985). And yet they turn out for training when it is offered. The stipend they receive during the month of training is part of the reason they do so. And then, for some, it is a route to a more satisfying role in the medical system. The PHCs "tend to use the trained dai as an intermediary with the village, to allow them to find prenatal or potential family-planning cases.." (Jeffery, p.276). Most dais, 83 percent in one study, like working with the PHC in this way, possibly because the official recognition they receive enhances their standing in the village.

The role of the dai in family planning is quite limited however and it seems destined to become even less significant in the future. Country wide, only a small fraction of deliveries are actually done by dais. Most are done by family members or older members of the village (Bhatia,1982). A great many dais, probably the large majority, have not been trained but this may not be as serious a matter as it might seem since, contrary to expectations, villagers continue to use untrained dais even when they might choose a trained one. Given the deep set beliefs regarding purity and pollution and the great social distance that certain kinds of human interactions demand in India, the lowly, untrained dai has her place. She is not likely to be replaced by her trained counterpart. Rather, the expansion of professional rural health services seems destined, in time, to eliminate her. In more developed villages, the dai is disappearing as a viable occupation and is being replaced by various forms of institutional care.

The Village Health Guide

In contrast to the "traditional birth attendants," the dais, the Village Health Guides (VHGs) are a recent addition to the rural health work force. Originally known as Community Health Workers (CHWs), the idea of putting an Indian version of the "barefoot doctor" in each village was proposed by the post-Emergency Janata government as part of an effort to bring health and family planning "closer to the people." Selection of candidate CHWs was to be made by the village panchayats to which the worker would return after a three month period of training. The panchayat nominees were then to be evaluated by PHC medical officers who were expected to make the final selection of a single candidate. In practise, medical officers usually prefer not to get involved in the selection process—not savoring the problems that might be caused by a rejected but well connected candidate—and thus do not ordinarily object when, as happens more than half the time (Narayana and Acharya), the village produces only a single nominee. Rather than involving the community in an earnest search for the best candidate for the job, selection tends to be a matter of patronage.

There have been other problems. The never-very-powerful Indian Medical Association raised strong objections to the scheme, seeing it as yet another threat to the quality of medical care in India. Challenges to the feasibility of the scheme came from other quarters also but it went ahead anyway, to a considerable extent because of its political appeal as a dependable source of patronage.

The concept of a village level health volunteer actually had been around a long time—at least since Nehru's day when the idea was "mooted" in a 1938 report of the National Planning Committee. It lay dormant for many years perhaps because of the stress on top down organization and professionalism advocated by the Bhore Committee and groups such as the Indian Medical Association. By the mid-seventies the time was ripe for its reappearance. Volunteers had been used with advantage in the much lauded privately run rural health project in Jamkhed, a rural area in Maharashtra. Equally important was the growing disenchantment with the western, professional model of health care. The criticism of writers like Ivan Illich were shared and expressed forcefully in India by such influential figures as V. Ramalingaswami, the longtime Director of the All India Institute of Medical Sciences and J.P. Naik, a certified Gandhian and the first head of the Indian Council for Social Science Research (Jeffery, p.228).

Despite its impressive backing and its political appeal, the scheme ran into problems from the outset due to the failure to think through the objectives and the precise role and responsibilities of the workers. Almost no thought was given to finding enough qualified trainers, to the selection of trainees, to their living arrangements during training, to their utilization upon returning to the village, to supervision, or to supplying them with basic medicines. Finally, the financial implications were not worked through for a scheme which, for salaries alone, would cost more than twice the total for current health expenditures (Jeffery, p.222).

Most CHVs were, and still are, men even though experience from the private sector suggested that women were generally more suitable. However, high rural unemployment put pressure on the panchayats to select males who, in any event, generally had a firmer claim on local patronage. As we shall see below, the issue of the sex of the CHV (now the VHG) has been a persistent and still largely unsettled one.

The unsettled nature of this program is reflected in the frequent changes in designation. The first change, from "community health worker" to "community health volunteer" was made in order to deflate the expectations of workers who assumed that they were being offered entry level jobs in the health service with full rights and entitlements. Apart from the visions of bureaucratic nirvana thus aroused, designation as a "worker" did seem to imply certain commitments which the Ministry was not prepared to assume.

The most recent change of designation came in 1980 and was almost purely political in intent. A voluntary, non-threatening approach to family planning was the necessary antidote for the ruthless actions taken during the Emergency. The introduction of the Community Health Worker (CHW) or the Community Health Volunteer (CHV) as primary agents of health care delivery and wrapping family planning in the cotton wool of health care was what the "spin doctors" of the time ordered. The new Janata government's Minister of Health, Raj Narain, a political maverick who had defeated Mrs Gandhi in her own constituency, made extension of CHVs to all villages his top priority. Narain may have picked up the idea from a 1975 report of a committee appointed by the health minister of that time, Dr. Karan Singh. Once returned to power in 1980, the Congress under Mrs Gandhi's leadership, found it hard to continue the scheme without changing its designation so as to rid it of its Janata origins. Thus the VHG was born.

Candidates selected for VHG training are given three month's of instruction at the local health center. During these three months they receive a relatively handsome stipend. On returning to their villages, after successfully finishing the course, they are then offered a modest monthly stipend as remuneration for the services they render on a part-time basis. Some of the more enterprising VHGs have capitalized on their training and their contacts with the health system by presenting themselves to the community as "government recognized doctors" and available to provide medical care for a fee. VHGs have displayed their enterprise in other directions as well. They have organized state level associations to press for better benefits and for recognition as bona fide medical personnel, claims that derive some credibility from the fact that they are seen as extensions of the regular health system.

VHGs are not supervised by the local panchayat, as was originally contemplated. Instead they work under the close supervision of the health and family welfare department. Like regular, full-time, health personnel, they are assigned targets for finding family planning acceptors. In fact, competition for family planning cases between VHGs and PHC staff is one of the main sources of friction between workers and "volunteers"—a relationship that has often been characterized by competition and confrontation rather than by cooperation and coordination (Narayana and Acharya). There is no evidence that the competition is healthy and results in better overall program performance; most commonly the argument is over the same cases.

In 1981 a policy shift occurred favoring the recruitment of women over men as VHGs. This was followed in 1987 by an abortive attempt to actually replace men with women volunteers. Instructions to the states ordering the implementation of this latter policy were subsequently withdrawn under effective political pressure but the idea did not go away. The latest policy variant is a "Revised Strategy for Family Welfare

Programme" announced by the Ministry in 1986. This envisions the creation of a village level women's volunteer corps, with one volunteer for every 60 families, to provide advice on health, nutrition, immunization and family. planning. Approximately 2 million women will have to be trained for this purpose. With characteristic disregard for small print, the Ministry, in launching this new scheme, did not make clear the differences between these new volunteers and the existing cadres of female health guides. Nor was it stated, perhaps for sound political considerations, whether this was a replacement for the earlier scheme—and thus another attempt to achieve the desired feminization of the village health work force—or whether this scheme was in addition to the old one. How and why the ratio of one volunteer to 60 households was chosen has not been explained.

Despite the criticism directed at the male VHG and the government's evident desire to replace him with a female counterpart, three major evaluation studies have concluded that male health guides are not only highly acceptable to villagers but appear to play a significant and positive role both in providing primary health care and in achieving family planning targets (National Institute of Health and Family Welfare, 1984). As noted above, however, there is evidence from private sector projects that in many respects, female workers do even better.

Health Auxiliaries

The shortage of rural health professionals is another difficult issue. Over the years various proposals have appeared to entice medical practitioners to rural areas or to develop a type who would settle and work there. Suggestions that indigenous medical practitioners be provided with additional training so that, as "licentiates," they could fill this need have been resisted repeatedly by the Indian Medical Association, which argues, somewhat piously and irrelevantly, that the rural population must enjoy the best of medical care and should not be served by "quacks," even retrained ones.

The idea for a type of paramedic able to deal with local health problems e.g. environmental sanitation and minor medical complaints, has been around at least since the 1950s. In 1954 the government proposed the creation of a cadre of health workers inspired, perhaps, by the Russian "feldsher," to render basic preventive and curative services at the village level. The proposal met the usual objections from professional medical circles that this was one more opening for quackery since it was widely believed that the temptation to go beyond the limits of their training and set up as private practitioners would prove irresistible (Jeffery p. 233). This objection had some credence since at one time the proposal was for a training period of three years and at another for a Bachelor of Science degree in public and maternal and child health (Jeffery, p. 231). Another complication, seized on by opponents, and also by some international bodies, was that sanitary inspectors were already in the field doing much of what the proposed new health worker was expected to do.

The scheme has had a long and involved history. Proposals were made by the Planning Commission to reduce the training in curative medicine to little more than "first aid" and provisions for supervision by a government doctor were put forward. It was not until 1975, when it became clear that any notions of basing the rural health service on retrained "hakims" or "vaids," the two major practitioners of indigenous medicine based respectively on Islamic and Vedic teaching, was not going anywhere, that it was decided to retrain the existing paramedical staff. By then a considerable number of such individuals had come into existence as workers in various disease specific programs, including family planning.

The time was right for the introduction of a health auxiliary. Some diseases, such as smallpox, were about to be vanquished and thus there were workers needing new assignments. In addition, the idea that health services should be integrated had made great headway. It was argued that a health worker with responsibilities for several health areas was more efficient and more acceptable in the community than the "unipurpose" worker. Field projects such as the one at Narangwal in the Punjab, suggested that combining responsibility for maternal and child health, nutrition, family planning and women's activities improved the quality and use of health services. The government's own tests of the idea in neighboring Harayana, in which personnel were deployed and supervised as provided in the health department's table of organization, reached the same conclusion. This was what the government needed to justify going ahead with the scheme, but as Jeffery points out after noting the many exceptions and failures to carry through with its implementation: "Integration within the health sector has thus far only been halfhearted; wider integration, with the work of nonhealth staff, has yet to be seriously considered" (Jeffery, p. 235). Jeffery is referring not only to the fact that there are still disease specific workers in the field, but in some areas District Medical Officers report to state and central disease-specific offices and as a result "place divergent pressure on their subordinates."

Converting workers from programs in public health, malaria eradication, immunization, maternal and child health and family planning into "multi-purpose" workers with responsibilities in each of these areas required new training programs and new training institutions. Beginning in 1974, seven Central Training Institutes, 47 Health and Family Welfare Training Centres and a few selected PHCs undertook the "reorientation" of the "uni-purpose" workers. It took more than a decade to complete training for all PHC personnel. Each worker now has a list of 46 jobs to perform arranged into 11 sets of activities. In practise, there is great variability in what actually gets attended to. As would be expected, workers respond to the pressures that arise in their particular situations and that come to them from higher authority.

Studies of the time workers spend at different tasks, subject as they are to recall error, show that most workers devote most of their time, on average two-thirds, to finding and persuading cases for sterilization. The remaining time, in the case of female workers, is spent on providing maternal and child health and immunization services and on record keeping. Male workers devote their time more to detecting and treating malaria cases and to public health (Narayana and Acharya). The large percentage of time given to finding cases for sterilization is a direct response to the constant pressure on these workers to meet their assigned targets. They derive greater satisfaction from certain other activities but the pressure is unrelenting. As a result, family planning is regarded virtually as a single purpose, vertical program. Under these conditions some observers have questioned the value of such integration since it is possible for a program like family planning to preempt the workers' time to such an extent that other areas are neglected (Sawhney).

The matter is not simply one of time allocation, however. At least one study (David and Narayana) has shown that workers who perform well in one area are superior performers in other areas also. This might suggest that the multi-purpose worker, if given a reasonably balanced set of work activities and good support, could effectively cover several health activities. Talk of reverting to the single purpose worker would seem to be premature.

Before giving up on the scheme, some of the widely recognized problems of the integrated scheme should be addressed. Among the most pressing, since it affects the morale of workers and has proven to disrupt program operations, is the failure to meet the worker's demand for uniform pay scales. Workers have come into the program with different educational qualifications, experience, previous wage levels and expectations regarding promotion. Now that they are all doing more or less the same job, there is a demand for uniform pay, obviously not at the lowest common level. This problem has been unattended for more than a decade both by the states and by the Centre Government.

Inaction on this matter has led workers to form unions, go on strike, and most ironic of all, resort informally to single lines of activity. As a result of administrative and management failures, the integration of health services has not been achieved nor has it had a proper, large scale trial.

The emphasis given to locating and "motivating" cases for sterilization, as we have said, monopolizes the time of health workers. It is even worse than that, however, since the common practise is to concentrate on a few likely acceptors to whom the worker makes repeated visits. If the worker is successful, additional time is taken to accompany the acceptor to wherever the operation is to be done, ordinarily a sterilization camp. This severely restricts the number of families that can be reached in a given period of time. A study in Uttar Pradesh (Mishra et al) found that the vast majority of families, especially the women, were not visited by health and family planning workers. The Second All India Survey confirmed these results more generally: out of nearly 12 thousand respondents only 11 percent had ever been contacted by a family planning worker (Khan and Prasad).

The baseline surveys conducted in connection with the Area Projects tell a similar story. Data from districts in which the USAID was involved showed that before the project went into operation only from 4 to 18 percent of women, depending on the state and district, who had given birth within the past 6 years had *ever* been visited by a family planning worker. The percentage of those who were visited *after* giving birth ranged from 3 to 12 percent. In Bihar, respondents who were aware (not necessarily through a home visit) either of the female worker or the supervisor ranged from a high of 47 percent in the most advanced district to a low of less that 1 percent in the poorest. Of the Bihari men and women in the study who had been sterilized, less than 6 percent of the men and less than 3 percent of the women considered the family planning worker to have been the "motivator."

It would be wrong to blame the field workers entirely for this poor showing. They work generally under quite adverse conditions. A major problem is transportation. The PHCs are seldom in a position to make transportation available to field workers and yet they are required as a rule to visit several villages in covering their assigned territory. In a place like Kerala, where about 90 percent of the rural population lives in villages of 10,000 or more population, this may not be a serious matter. Such villages are large enough to qualify for a PHC and for a sub-centre and thus services are near at hand and the population highly accessible for home visiting. Contrast that with the problem states of the north, Bihar, Uttar Pradesh, Rajasthan, and Madhya Pradesh, where the rural population is widely dispersed thus giving the health workers an extensive catchment area in which to work. Bose has assembled 1981 Census data to show that the proportion of rural population living in large clusters of 10,000 or more is around 4 percent for Bihar and less than one percent for the other three states (Bose, op cit. p 152; see also Narayana). The enormous disparity in the physical accessibility of health service is underscored by differences in state road networks. In Kerala all villages with 1000 or more population are connected by road to other settlements. By contrast, in the northern states of Bihar, Madhya Pradesh, Rajasthan and Uttar Pradesh, which together make up 40 percent of India's population, less than 2 out of five small villages (under 1500 population) and less than 2 out of 3 villages above that size are so connected with the outside world.

The reach of the program is limited also, as we have seen, by the intense pressure on workers to secure family planning acceptors. This forces them to concentrate their efforts on a few households where they believe they may find ready sterilization clients. Furthermore the health worker gets little help from the local community. The "Orientation Camps," which are meant to build rapport with local leaders and village elders, spend much of their time pressuring those in attendance for assistance in meeting family planning targets.

The mania for target achievement has truly diverted the health and family planning worker from playing the kind of role that enthusiasts for integration had in mind. Targets for sterilization and IUD insertions are assigned to health workers, to VHGs and to personnel from other departments that come into contact with the population, e.g. agriculture, education, revenue, and social welfare. The allocation of targets to departments other than the health department is often done by the District Collector or the District Development Officer. These are then handed down to individuals working in these departments. At each level the targets tend to be increased on the theory that added pressure will increase performance. Instances have been reported of more target being assigned than there were eligible couples. There then is likely to follow a kind of feeding frenzy as workers from different agencies search out cases within a limited and overlapping area. The same couple is likely to be visited by personnel from different agencies so intense is the competition for cases. Credit for "motivating" an acceptor is frequently claimed by more than one worker and sometimes is resolved in the presence of the physician just as the operation is about to proceed.

The competition to meet assigned targets has little to do with the meager finders fees that are awarded. The "motivator" receives Rs. 10 for each sterilization case and Rs.2 for an IUD acceptor. Annually workers average about 10 sterilization cases which means that their incentive payments would amount to about 10 percent of their monthly salary. Workers often spend much more than that on providing tea and snacks for the acceptor and the entourage of relatives that make the journey to the camp. It is little wonder that clients frequently complain of being left to their own devices after the operation, the worker showing little further interest. The root of the workers competitive behavior is to be found, rather, in the fact that those who fail to meet their targets can expect rough treatment ranging from insulting comments directed toward them at department meetings to transfer and, in extreme cases, to withholding of pay. Such punishment must be avoided at all costs and so various practises have developed to provide the worker some protection. For example, in Tamil Nadu, a market has developed whereby workers with excess cases can put them up for bid. Prices fluctuate seasonally as the pressure on workers for cases intensifies toward the end of the fiscal year (David and Narayana). Low performance workers may spend up to a month's salary to get the required number of cases even, in some instances, making payments to clients willing to become acceptors. Acceptors who come forward on their own without any prompting or assistance from health workers are nevertheless claimed by the first worker they encounter.

It is virtually impossible to make reasonable estimates of the productivity of health workers even in the simplest terms of relating family planning clients obtained in a given period to the wages paid to health and family planning workers. If the total number of sterilizations and IUD insertions are all attributed to the efforts of health and family planning workers, their productivity, so measured, works out for 1983–84 to around 2.4 sterilizations per month and a little over 1 case for IUD. Even this modest performance is grossly overstated since it assumes that supervisory workers (they have targets to meet also), workers from other departments, VHGs, dais and Private Voluntary Organizations (they have target assigned if they receive government money) bring in no cases.

It can be objected that workers don't spend all their time on family planning and that this should be allowed for in assessing their productivity. But the fact is that they spend probably two-thirds of their time rounding up family planning acceptors and can be fairly credited with no more than 50 percent of the reported cases (David and Narayana). On these assumptions, the family planning productivity of these workers who carry the primary target burden as the program is now set up, figures out to a little over 14 sterilizations and around 7 IUD cases *per year*. Even making allowance for time spent on other activities, this is hardly an impressive level of output.

The nature of the transactions that occur between workers and villagers, the "encounter," is a subject that has received some study (Gupta and Singh; Rao; Narayana; Reddy and Narayana), but the results do not seem to have attracted much notice from program managers. Similarly, the nature of the relationships between male and female workers, between workers and supervisors and between health workers and workers from other departments, are known to be problematic for the smooth functioning of the program but knowledge about them is essentially anecdotal. There is evidently a lack of supportive interaction among program functionaries. Some of the relationships are in fact exploitative, as when supervisors "snatch away" cases from their subordinates. There are other problems that deserve to be addressed such as the dilution of supervision by time spent chasing targets and the poor provisions for advancement. Practically all supervisors, regardless of years in service or efficiency ratings, can expect to leave government service in the same grade. One cannot hope to go for the brass ring; one can only aspire not to be unhorsed.

At this level of operation, from the district level down to the PHC and the village, the program can be said to be misdirected, limited in outreach and of low productivity. These defects are widely recognized but, unfortunately, proposed remedies tend to be of the armchair variety. There is a great need for genuine experimentation with alternate ways of providing family planning services and interesting the public in them. The search should not be for a new, uniform strategy with uniform standards of performance but for varied strategies adapted to the diversity of the country.

The Medical Officer

At the present time each PHC serves a population of 100,000 or more, an entire development block. Plans are to convert one out of three of these to Community Health Centres which will offer specialized services. Some of the wealthier states have already put these plans into operation while others lag far behind. It is estimated that it will take about ten years to install the plan in all parts of the country. Questions have been raised about the likely success of the CHCs which will have to face competition from better equipped, more fully staffed nearby hospitals. Specialized curative services require more by way of support staff and facilities than is so far envisioned for the CHCs.

The PHC usually has three medical officers, the most senior of which is the officer-in-charge. A revamped sub-block level PHC will have one medical officer, a community health officer, an extension educator plus male and female health assistants, a lab technician and a statistician. For many years the most discussed problem concerning the operation of the PHC was the difficulty of recruiting physicians willing to serve in rural areas. With the great expansion in the number of medical schools and the output of new doctors, the lucrative urban markets for medical services have become crowded and highly competitive. There are 106 medical schools in the country. In 1983–84 the institutions turned out about 12,000 physicians plus another 2,600 who obtained post-graduate degrees.

The number of medical professionals registered with Employment Exchanges has increased markedly. In 1984 there were almost 20,000 medical professionals on the live registers of the employment exchanges. In many states the number of government positions for physicians is less than the number of applicants. There is now a fair degree of competition for openings for physicians in the government's rural health service to the point that court challenges over hiring decisions are not uncommon.

Getting a son or daughter into medical school is a major preoccupation of many parents. Physicians generally enjoy high status and have excellent earning prospects. Young male doctors, moreover, command a handsome price as prospective bridegrooms. For most graduates the goal is a career in curative medicine and in specialties in demand in urban areas. The health service, on the other hand, seeks physicians oriented toward preventive medicine who are interested in serving in rural areas. While some very fine physicians are attracted to the kind of opportunity offered by government service, it is doubtful whether a sufficient number of physicians would be available for such jobs were it not for the abundance of physicians looking for work.

Physicians posted for rural service to PHC or other out-of-the-way facilities usually have their eye on the main chance as urban practitioners. For many there is a large and painful gap between what they do as medical officers in the rural health service and what they would prefer to do if they had the opportunity.

There have been efforts to reduce this gap by placing greater emphasis on preventive medicine in medical school curricula and by exposing medical students to the health problems of rural populations. There is little evidence that these efforts have made many converts. When medical officers were asked in a study conducted in Maharastra to list the organizational priorities by which they were expected to operate, they listed them, in order, as family planning, MCH, immunization, public health and, in last place, curative services (David and Narayana). When asked for their own preferences they listed curative medical care first followed by MCH, immunization and, as low priorities, public health and family planning. Most important, the survey found that the physician's own priorities were determining. They spent almost half their time on curative services, almost another 40 percent on administration, leaving less than 15 percent for all other programs (David and Narayana). Other studies have found (see for example Misra et al) that many physicians posted to Primary Health Centres

> devote all their energies to achieving a transfer to a more desirable center, visiting the district or state headquarters for long periods to lobby and persuade senior staff to change their posting. Staff members may disappear on long leaves until they receive a better posting or they may be moved to other positions. These are two of the means by which posts may be filled-up, although the staff may be almost permanently absent. A possibly extreme example is provided by a study of a primary health center in Uttar Pradesh in 1977–78, during the post-emergency collapse of the family planning program, when five staff members spent 75 percent of their time absent or on personal business (Jeffery, p.266).

Faced with the conflict between professional and personal interests on the one hand and organizational goals on the other and with the high hopes of his or her family as a goad to ambition, a PHC medical officer will often seek private patients, freely using the resources of the Centre in the process. This is most easily arranged by the chief medical officer. Denial of similar opportunities to junior medical officers is a major source of conflict within the medical staff. Some states have passed legislation to curb private practise by government physicians. Others have offered "non-practise allowances" but these have been paltry sums compared to the income that can be derived from private practise. As might be expected there is pervasive agitation for increases in these allowances. In the meanwhile, private practise continues to flourish.

One consequence of the high rates of absenteeism and time devoted to seeing private patients, is that regular patients visiting the PHC may get very little time with the doctor. Studies of this problem go back some years when it was found that the median time spent with the doctor was 2 minutes or less (Murthy and Parker, 1973). According to one qualified commentator, "average times are not likely to have risen since then" (Jeffery, p. 267). With an efficient staff of health technicians and a well designed protocol for handling patients, a physician can do a lot in a brief encounter with a patient. But this seems not to be the way it works. An observation of prenatal consultations in Varanasi district of Uttar Pradesh, revealed that women were never weighed nor were hemoglobin levels determined; instruments were not sterilized and blood pressures not always recorded. Other studies uncovered inappropriate prescribing and little or no advice given by the doctor to the patient (Jeffery, ibid).

Before laying all the blame for these deplorable practises on the doctor, who must nevertheless receive much of it, it must be appreciated that most of the PHC budget goes for salaries, leaving inadequate sums for patient care. Some estimates put the average drug budget at around Rs.1 (ca. 6 cents) per patient per year (Jeffery, ibid). In addition there are often long delays in the release of funds for drugs and a supply system so inefficient that the typical PHC does not have on hand many of the basic medicines it needs. As a result patients needing any but the most common and cheapest medicines are expected to buy them on the market. The one exception is that supplies required for sterilization operations, which are provided from a special fund, are generally available (Jeffery, p.268).

Relationships between the medical officers on the one hand and the supervisors and other health workers on the other, are apt to suffer from wide differences in social origins, caste, education, income and opportunities for advancement in the health system. The enormous social distance between these two groups often results in a breakdown of any semblance of teamwork. Physicians are likely to be blind to significant differences between supervisors and workers which undermines working relationships on that level. Communication is often minimal across this status gap, except when necessitated by crisis situations. At those times interaction is likely to feature the excessive use of authority, thus planting seeds for future friction and misunderstanding. Most regrettable of all, perhaps, is that the medical officer by his high-handed way of dealing with his staff, burns one of the few bridges he has to understanding the local community and adapting his programs, in so far as he is permitted to do so, to local needs. There are, as one might expect, a few heroic exceptions to the picture presented here.

Medical officers are isolated professionally as well. They have few opportunities for any kind of "continuing education" and have virtually no access to professional journals. Thus they have difficulty in keeping up with medical advances and are susceptible to taking at face value stray bits of medical information or opinion that come along with no chance for independent verification (Pathfinders, India, 1983). Medical bulletins, newsletters, and workshops all bearing the imprimatur of recognized medical authority could do much to overcome this professional isolation of the PHC doctor.

The setting in which service providers operate obviously makes a significant difference in how well they function. For most family planning personnel that setting is either the PHC or a sub-centre (see Appendix A), the principal facilities available to the rural population. Urban communities have a wider range of choice. Private organizations offering contraceptive services generally are located in urban areas although, again, there are some notable exceptions. Perhaps the most effective settings for delivering family planning services are the post partum centres attached to urban hospitals. These centres in 1987 accounted for 15 percent of urban acceptors, primarily tubectomy and IUD. The medical personnel at Post Partum Centres, who have many duties other than delivering contraception (e.g. performing more than 2 in 5 of the total annual number of medically approved abortions (MOHFW 1986–87 Year Book, Tables D.20 and J1.4), represent only 3 percent of urban medical service personnel involved in family planning.

On up the Line

The layer of authority immediately above the PHC is the district. The district has always been a focal level of administration in the Indian administrative system. Usually a district is headed by a member of the civil service known with confusing variability either as the "collector" or the "magistrate," depending on whether revenue or judicial functions are being referred to. While this person is clearly the most powerful official in the district, his power is shared to some extent with representatives of other departments. The idea that the magistrate's power should be checked and balanced by that of other officials goes back to Governor General Cornwallis who argued against an all powerful representative of central power in the Mughal style. In some states the collector has been confined to attending to revenue collection and law and order. For the purposes of district development there may be a District Development Officer (DDO) in charge of all development programs, including health and family planning. It is this official who feels such pressure as there may be from the Chief Minister of the State or Ministers responsible for particular activities such as health and family planning. This is the official who apportions family planning targets among the various departments under his charge. In states that have not so limited the responsibilities of the collector, he is the one responsible for development programs.

Whereas PHC organization is fairly uniform across the country, district organization varies from state to state. In addition to the question of the collectors "span of control," there are also differences in the way district program officers function. In some states, program officers are responsible only to their departmental superiors at the state level and concern themselves only with their special subject, be it malaria, leprosy, tuberculosis, family planning, curative services or public health. This puts a tremendous load on the PHC supervisors who must somehow deal with the demands of several programs. Field workers often have to contend with contradictory instructions which come to them from several directions.

To ease this situation some states have created "multi-purpose" district officers to take care of family planning, public health and medical services. Other programs operate as before. This "solution" has not been wholly successful since the authority delegated to the "multi-purpose" officer has sometimes been limited so that his role becomes more advisory than directive, a situation which has led to clashes with other program officers and with the Chief District Health Officer who is responsible for the full range of health programs. To get around this problem, some states have lodged the "multi-purpose" officer at the subdivisional level, between the district and the PHC, but unfortunately have failed to provide the resources necessary to do the job.

Other schemes have been tried, for example, dividing districts into health subunits, abolishing the position of chief district health officer and letting the head of each subunit deal up the line with program officers at the directorate level. This system appears to have aided in the decentralization of control and provides avenues of advancement for medical officers. However, until there is reform higher up in the system, gains from district level reorganization will be limited. This is not to say that there have not been some encouraging developments. As we saw earlier, where district administration has been made accountable to elected self government, the Zila Parishads, better planning, implementation and program monitoring has resulted. Under these conditions, in Maharashtra, Karnataka, Andhra Pradesh, Kerala, Gujarat, West Bengal and Tamil Nadu, programs have gained the support of local politicians with the result that the reception of family planning by villagers has perceptibly improved.

While there are differences among the states in the way development activities are handled, the states, by and large, have taken initiatives only when pressure is applied from above. The main axis runs between activities at the district (and subdistrict) level and central policy makers. There is the further problem that at the Center all is not as it should be. The continual transfer of ministers and secretaries and portfolio shifts within the organization have led to drift and uncertainty. Moreover, there is a debilitating overlap of functional responsibility, inadequate staffing in critical sections and excess in others, uncertain delegation of authority, poor interorganizational communication, and a lack of information about many essential matters. There has been no attempt to introduce at the central level the analog of the "multi-purpose" officer favored at lower levels. Each program officer at the central ministry works in relative isolation.

The Ministry has called upon outside consultants for advise on what to do about these problems which are well recognized by Ministry officials. But the situation persists. The system in its present form is deeply entrenched. Strong, committed, leadership will be needed to overcome the resistance which would inevitably arise from attempts to change it.

5

Program Performance

Proving the Pudding

The title of this chapter is deceptively simple. A program has many facets to it. What these are and how they might be measured is not immediately obvious. Students of the problem have isolated at least four broad areas or program components that together make up what has come to be called "program effort" (Lloyd and Ross, 1989). The first relates to putting in place the facilities and organization needed for delivering family planning services. A second component is defined by activities that inform prospective clients about the program and attract them to it. A third component has to do with the gathering of information needed to guide the program and assess its progress. Finally, if a program is physically in place, people know about it and are encouraged to use it and if provision has been made to measure the results, there remains the question of the content of the program, i.e. the services actually offered and their availability (Bongaarts et al, 1990, Lapham and Mauldin, 1985).

Measuring these various components is not an easy matter but it is possible to rank national programs as to the strength of the efforts made to reduce fertility. According to such reckonings, India is classified among countries with moderately strong programs. "Strong" does not mean that the program is as good as it ought to be. It means merely that on the specific items that have been used to measure the four program components it does better than many other programs. The Indian program, for example, is stronger by these measures than, say, Pakistan's or Egypt's. But, as we have gone to some length to demonstrate, there is much that is wrong with the Indian program.

"Performance" too presents conceptual and measurement problems. In a proximate sense, one thinks of the response to the program in terms of contraceptive prevalence. There are, of course, steps that come before that, for example, measures of whether the program is being implemented as planned. Then there are less proximate indicators that measure the impact of the program in preventing births. Since, as we have seen, the prevalence of contraceptive use has emerged as a dominant factor in Indian fertility, we will be concerned here largely with that measure of performance.

Performance Evaluation

The favorite statistic used by the Ministry of Health and Family Welfare for evaluating performance is the percentage of assigned targets that have been achieved. These statistics are compiled and published by year, by method and by state and fill pages in the annual Year Books put out by the Ministry. Another statistic that gets a lot of attention is the estimate of "births averted" by the use of contraception. This figure is a mechanical calculation of the births that might have occurred had it not been for the use of contraception, given the methods in use and their presumed efficiencies.

Somewhat more useful are the data on contraceptive prevalence—the percentage of married couples using contraception. These data are presented in two forms: the percentage of couples using any method of contraception and the percentage of couples using contraception "effectively," i.e. the same group discounted for the assumed effectiveness of the methods they are using. To illustrate, in 1986–87 slightly more than 40 percent of couples were using some form of contraception. Those who were sterilized were assumed to be completely protected but the number of those using other methods was discounted in terms of the birth averting efficiency of the method they were using. IUD users were discounted by a little over 6 percent whereas users of "other methods" received a deep discount of more than 40 percent. Evaluation of the program has consisted, for the most part, of compiling these statistics coming from the field, with occasional, ad hoc, investigations into their validity.

There are reasons to question the validity of some of the data put forward to show the gains made by the program. Generally the data on sterilizations appear reasonably accurate but data on other methods are more questionable. For example in a rural district in Maharashtra which had reported a total of 96 users of the Copper-T, an advanced design IUD, only 5 users and 12 discontinued users could be traced. Tracing is difficult in India because many people do not have locatable addresses and because the address information recorded by field workers is often incomplete. Nevertheless, to find less than 1 in 5 of recorded contraceptive users raises questions about possible falsification of data—for which there are many strong inducements.

In considering the question of the validity of data on contraceptive use, some have been comforted by the passable agreement of the data derived from service statistics and data obtained from sample surveys carried out by the Operations Research Group (ORG), a private survey research organization. Total use, as estimated by MOHFW, is actually somewhat higher than shown by the survey, (Table 5.1), the difference being due entirely to greater reported use of the IUD. Lacking sampling errors for the survey, it is not possible to analyze these differences satisfactorily, but it is likely that major factors are the estimates of discontinuation rates employed by MOHFW statisticians as well as inflation in the initial recording of acceptors of temporary methods. Reluctance of survey respondents to admit to using temporary methods is another possibility. Both sets of numbers are consistent with a CPR in the vicinity of 40 percent which, as noted in Chapter II, is consistent with a TFR in the neighborhood of 4.0 to 4.5.

TABLE 5.1   Contraceptive Use by Method and Data Source, 1987

Method	ORG Survey	MOHFW (Percent Using)	Difference
	(1)	(2)	(1–2)
Sterilization	29.6	28.9	+0.7
IUD	1.9	5.5	-3.6
Condom	5.2	4.2	+1.0
Pill	1.3	1.5	-0.2
All Modern Methods	38.0	40.1	-2.1
All Methods	43.0	44.3[a]	-1.3

[a]Total for All Modern Methods is the sum of those methods listed above. Elsewhere MOHFW shows total use of the methods it distributes, all of which are "modern methods" as 44.3. Adding MTPs would do little to reconcile this difference.

Source: ORG Survey 1990, Table 7.3. The numerators of the MOHFW estimates have been adjusted for attrition among acceptors but not for the presumed effectiveness of the method; denominators are projections of age proportions in the 1971 and 1981 Censuses adjusted also for proportions married. Survey information is for April 1987; MOHFW "provisional" estimates for March 31, 1987.

TABLE 5.2   Percentage Using Modern Methods by State and Source

State	All Modern Methods		Sterilization	
	Survey	OHFW	Survey	MOHFW
North				
Haryana	52.0	72.1	38.0	30.6
Punjab	66.0	78.3	36.0	33.9
Rajasthan	29.0	29.9	23.0	21.3
Uttar				
Pradesh	26.0	31.4	17.0	15.3
East				
Bihar	29.0	23.3	21.0	18.3
Orissa	43.0	39.5	34.0	30.6
West Bengal	40.0	31.3	30.0	27.2
West				
Gujarat	47.0	57.9	38.0	38.0
Maharashtra	53.0	57.7	43.0	42.9
South				
Andhra				
Pradesh	49.0	41.2	46.0	32.6
Karnataka	47.0	43.9	39.0	33.2
Kerala	66.0	48.5	57.0	39.0
Tamil Nadu	46.0	54.5	37.0	39.5
All India	38.0	40.1	29.6	28.9

Source: ORG 1990, Tables 7.3, 7.4, 7.5, 7.6. MOHFW, Yearbook,1986–87.

Thus on the national level there appears to be reasonable agreement. Somewhat disconcerting, however, are the data on total use of "modern methods" for individual states. Even recognizing that the survey data are more subject to random error at lower levels of aggregation, the size of some of the differences are such as to raise suspicions about the validity of official data on contraceptive use (Table 5.2).

No single pattern of difference emerges from a comparison of contraceptive prevalence rates returned from these two sources. The MOHFW rates are substantially higher in five states—Haryana, Punjab, Gujarat, Maharashtra, and Tamil Nadu. The differences appear to be due to different levels reported for temporary methods. The survey found the use of sterilization to be in rough agreement with the Ministry's figures. In four states—West Bengal, Andhra Pradesh, Karnataka, and Kerala— the survey found significantly more contraceptive use than was registered by MOHFW. The differences can be attributed largely to the greater use of sterilization discovered by the survey. This, in turn, is explained to some extent by post-partum tubectomies performed on educated, urban women in private facilities that are not recognized by the government and so do not report to state or local governments.

There is not much good information on this subject, but it is widely believed among program administrators and other observers that over-reporting is on the increase. Sterilizations being better documented and more traceable, overreporting is most likely in the case of temporary methods. Pressure to achieve targets and competition between the states for performance awards are two reasons often cited for inflated reports in the number of contraceptive users.

Evaluation of the family planning program is generally made in terms of these fallible quantitative indicators. Evaluation of the qualitative aspects of the program tends to be ad hoc, if done at all. The poor quality of services provided by the program is one of its most serious shortcomings yet the family planning bureaucracy has insulated itself from an objective assessment of program quality. When reports emanate from different quarters concerning deficiencies and abuses—medical complications, method failures, etc.—there is seldom an inquiry into the matter. Similarly, charges that performance data are being manipulated go uninvestigated, since to pry into such questions is something seasoned bureaucrats know not to do.

Trends in the CPR

According to government statistics, the use of contraception has more than tripled since 1970 when less than 12 percent of couples took such precautions (Table 5.3). The increase has come in three discernible waves. From 1970 up to the time of the Emergency in 1975, the CPR increased gradually, primarily because of the advent in the early 1970s of sterilization camps—the method responsible for most of the increase. Then came the Emergency with its forced recruitment of vasectomy cases. The CPR, which had stopped growing, increased by 16 percent in 1975–76 and by 35 percent in 1976–77. All of this increase was attributable to sterilization.

The reported CPR remained sluggish until 1982–83 after which it began to rise by 2 to 3 percentage points a year. All methods contributed to this upward trend but, taking the reported figures at face value, non-terminal methods showed the greatest relative gains (Table 5.3).

Sterilization

The Indian family planning program has long been known as a sterilization program. For developing countries generally, sterilization

TABLE 5.3   Percent of Couples Using Contraception, by Method, 1970–1971 to
1986–1987

Year	Sterilization	IUD	Other Methods	Total
1970–1971	8.1	1.4	2.1	11.5
1971–1972	9.7	1.4	2.4	13.5
1972–1973	12.2	1.2	2.4	15.8
1973–1974	12.2	1.1	3.0	16.3
1974–1975	12.6	1.0	2.4	16.1
1975–1976	14.2	1.1	3.4	18.7
1976–1977	20.7	1.1	3.4	25.3
1977–1978	20.1	0.9	3.0	24.0
1978–1979	19.9	1.0	3.1	23.9
1979–1980	19.9	1.0	2.7	23.6
1980–1981	20.1	1.1	3.3	24.4
1981–1982	20.7	1.2	3.8	25.7
1982–1983	22.0	1.4	4.9	28.4
1983–1984	23.7	2.3	6.8	32.7
1984–1985	24.9	3.0	7.7	35.6
1985–1986	26.5	3.9	8.3	38.7
1986–1987	27.9	4.8	8.0	40.7
1987–1988	28.9	5.5	5.7	40.1
1989 (Survey)	31.3	1.9	6.7	39.9

Source: Ministry of Health and Family Planning, Family Welfare Program in
India, Year Books, 1981–82 to 1986–87. ORG, 1990, Table 7.1.

accounts for 40 percent or less, usually much less, of contraceptive use
(Nortman, 1985). Although the Indian authorities are working to change
the complexion of the program, sterilization still provides 70 percent of
the "effective" protection enjoyed by Indian couples who use contraception. In some states sterilization accounts for over 80 percent of current
use. Sterilization is a universally recognized method even in rural areas
(Table 5.4). Indian couples themselves, except for more sophisticated
urbanites, tend to think of sterization when they think of contraception.
A national survey that sampled opinion before the recent push for non-
terminal methods, found that 80 percent of non-contracepting couples
who were planning to use birth control sometime in the future said they
would opt for sterilization (Khan and Prasad, 1983). To some extent the
salient position of sterilization in the program can be understood by the
method's compatibility with a centralized, target oriented, have-done-
with-it, mode of operation. Sterilization also is the method that the
Government promotes, above all others, by incentives that, in a poor
country like India, certainly do not go unnoticed.

TABLE 5.4   Awareness of Contraceptive Methods by Residence

Residence	Sterilization		IUD	Condom	Pill	Rhythm	C.I.[a]
	Male	Female					
Urban	92	97	77	84	78	38	25
Rural	88	94	48	60	54	23	14
Total	89	95	55	66	60	27	17

[a]Coitus interruptus, withdrawal

Source: ORG, 1990, Table 5.1.

To break out of this mold will require a substantial effort to educate the population about alternatives to sterilization and to develop a program capable of delivering them. An initial hurdle to be overcome is the lesser awareness of alternative methods of contraception. Less than half of married rural women interviewed admitted any knowledge of the IUD. Awareness of the condom and the pill is somewhat more widespread but still over one third of rural women profess to be ignorant of the condom and nearly half say that they don't know about the pill.

Knowledge of how these methods are used is even more limited. Surveys conducted in some of the poorer districts of Gujarat, Maharashtra, Haryana, Punjab and Himachal Pradesh reveal a similar lack of awareness of anything except sterilization (Office of the Registrar General, 1985; IIPS, 1985). Data from these studies show reported awareness of different methods to be highly variable. Although data of this kind are sensitive to subtle differences in the way the interviews are conducted, they leave no doubt as to a widespread lack of familiarity with methods such as the IUD and the pill. Out of 13 districts studied, awareness of the IUD was well below 50 percent in all but one. In half of the districts it was less than 25 percent. The pill fared even more poorly. Awareness of this method ranged from 2 percent to 26 percent; in over half of the districts, it was less than 10 percent. Familiarity with sterilization is not surprising given its stormy history as part of the Indian family planning program.

Sterilization received a strong push in the early 1970s with the introduction of mass vasectomy camps. World attention was drawn to the highly organized activities of a Collector in Ernakulam district of Kerala state—later to become Minister of State for Family Welfare in Delhi—who brought in villagers by the truckload for vasectomy. The vasectomy camp idea spread quickly to other regions and, as a consequence, sterilizations among married couples rose two percentage points a year during this introductory period.

There followed a period of stagnation as the problems associated with the hurried introduction of this new approach came to be known. The intensive, assembly line processing of patients in which doctors competed to outdo each other in the number of operations performed proved objectionable. Interest in sterilization camps was dampened further as stories of high failure rates circulated. Whether failure was because of poor surgical technique or because patients were not properly warned that sterility was not instantaneous, the procedure got a bad name among many potential clients.

While the Ernakulam camps were reported to be models of efficient organization (Soni), these conditions were not always duplicated elsewhere. The strain on organizational capacity at times passed the breaking point in handling the large volume of patients and almost nowhere was there adequate follow-up. Another possible factor that is often mentioned was concern over possible loss of virility and the invitation to marital infidelity absent the evidence of a philandering witnessed by a fetus delicti. These early signs of difficulty went unrecognized by those who might have been able to take corrective action. As a result, the number of vasectomy cases fell sharply to pre-camp levels where it remained until the Emergency which fell upon the country a few years later.

Unhindered by the normal restraints of democratic procedure, the Emergency set about attending, at times in almost military fashion, to some of the nation's persistent problems, among which was rapid population growth. With few models to chose from in its own experience, the choice of those in charge was to step up the pace of recruiting acceptors for sterilization, vasectomy in particular. In sheer quantitative terms the program was a success; in almost every other sense it was a disaster. At the zenith of the Emergency's "achievements" in population control, 1 out of 5 couples had been sterilized. But there it stopped. It was not until 1982, that the percentage of sterilized couples again began to ascend, this time because of a growth in female sterilization. Vasectomy did not recover as a popular procedure.

The return to power of an apparently chastened Indira Gandhi ready again to take up the cause of birth control, this time with much pious utterance about its voluntary nature, coincided with the appearance of a new technology for female sterilization, the laparoscope. This new device, imported from the west, made tubectomy as quick as vasectomy and, in the right hands, was safe and effective. With its long established weakness for new technology, the administrators of the program endorsed this new technique with enthusiasm. It was accepted eagerly also by many physicians and by 1983–84, nearly half (49.4 percent) of tubal ligations were performed with the laparoscope. The popularity of laparoscopy fell after that but appears to have claimed a stable share of around 40 percent of the market for tubectomy.

It is quite common for new products to retreat somewhat from the high levels of acceptance they enjoy on first being introduced. Undoubtedly this is part of the reason for the slight sag after 1983–84 in acceptance of laparoscopy. But there is evidently more to the story than that since in a few states the fall back was dramatic: in Andrha Pradesh from over 30 percent of total tubectomies to 10 percent; in Bihar from 61 percent to 47 percent; in Orissa from 40 to 22 percent; in Karnataka from 38 to 26 percent; in Maharashtra from 32 to 22 percent; in Punjab from 63 to 34 percent; in Tamil Nadu from 56 to 31 percent. Perhaps the more relevant question is not why laparoscopy lost popularity in some states, but why its initial gains were so short lived; why it didn't continue on to sweep the field in, what was then, a growing market for tubectomy.

Some small scale studies are suggestive. For example, in Madhya Pradesh, a camp held in a town hospital had 17 failures out of a total of 19 laparoscopic sterilizations. There have been similar reports from other areas. A study in Rajasthan by the same group of investigators from the respected Indian Institute of Management, Ahmedabad, encountered widespread complications associated with laparoscopic sterilization. Medical officers in that state put the failure rate at different facilities between 5 and 30 percent. Another problem was met with in Bihar where 10 percent of the scopes were found to be out of order as were a number of autoclaves and sterilizers.

In spite of these widely discussed problems, none of the states has seriously looked into the reasons for high failure rates or for the higher than expected rates of complication and occasional death. Instead, the tendency, in most cases, is to suppress information and keep cases of failure out of the records. Had early attention been given to quality control, to proper maintenance of equipment, to better patient care and follow-up and, perhaps most importantly, to making the physician accountable for the patients well being during and after the operation, the laparoscope might now enjoy a better reputation and occupy a more prominent place in the program.

Non-terminal Methods

The disappointment with laparoscopy as a new method that it was hoped would carry the program to new heights of achievement together with the knockout blow administered to vasectomy by the Emergency led officials to look again at ways to increase interest in other methods of contraception.

Attention turned to methods commonly referred to, somewhat misleadingly, as "spacing methods." These are not only different methods but methods that are appropriate for young couples with fewer children than they might ultimately want. There is an untapped market here as only 16 percent of all couples using contraception are under thirty years of age (Srinivasan, 1987). The average number of living children among sterilized couples remains stuck at around 3.5 (MOHFW, Year Book 1986–87, Table F 3.1) and the hoped for spread of sterilization to young couples does not appear to be materializing fast enough to make any real difference. Add to this the stalled birth rate and it becomes obvious that new strategies are needed. "Spacing methods" are the logical and, except for abortion which has never been popular in India, the only choice.

In time honored fashion, a Committee was established, this one for Promotion of Spacing Methods of Contraception. In a report submitted in 1987, the Committee recommended, in addition to greater prominence for spacing methods, a list of what by now are standard items in such documents: "reorientation of service providers," "community involvement," "community based distribution." Among "spacing methods," the Committee gave pride of place to the IUD and the pill.

The IUD

As with other technological innovations, the IUD was introduced in 1965 without adequate provision for long term customer satisfaction. It had an immediate and encouraging reception from the public. In the year in which it was added to the program and in the year following, the IUD accounted for 40 percent of new acceptors and for the first and only time, exceeded the number of sterilizations. Rejection followed just as swiftly. Again the familiar pattern asserted itself: rather than fix what might be wrong with the program, the Ministry backed away and turned its attention to another new idea, this time the "social marketing" of condoms.

The problems with the IUD that needed attention, according to studies done at the time (Agarwal, 1967) included the usual complaints about quality of service and an unusually high rate of "discomfort" reported by women using the device. In contrast to experience in other countries, where half of the IUD acceptors may complain of discomfort in the first month of use, 70 percent of Indian women did so. After 12 months of use complaints of discomfort generally fall off to an almost negligible 5 to 6 percent but in India, 40 percent of the women who were still using the IUD at the end of the first year voiced such complaints. As the result of poorly organized services and poor care and follow-up of patients, the Indian program experienced unusually high rates of expulsion and removal.

The device used in this early experience with the IUD was the Lippes Loop which is manufactured in India. Currently the device of choice in the program is the Copper-T (Cu-T), an advanced type of IUD which has taken over that market. In Maharashtra, more than 80 percent of the IUDs being installed are of this new variety. There are plans to begin manufacture of the Cu-T, which is now imported, in both the private and public sectors.

Oral Contraception

Unlike the IUD, oral contraception has never had a large scale trial in India in which the government could be said to be unambiguously behind it. When it was first tried some years ago, the government took a cautious stance because of the unsettled scientific opinion then prevailing regarding safety and side effects. The pill was made a prescription drug. While this is a much less inhibiting restriction for a determined user in India than a similar requirement might be in many other places, this action plus the emphasis put on contraindications to use put the physician, who often knew little about the scientific questions involved, in a position where caution appeared the sensible course to take. Because the pill was an "ethical" drug, Government regulations required that it be advertised only in medical journals. Altogether an inauspicious beginning.

Resistance among physicians, who got little or no help from the authorities in informing themselves on the issues, the prescription barrier and, more importantly, the lack of promotion, kept the pill confined to an insignificant role in the program. If this were not enough to ruin its prospects, the conviction among many professionals and lay persons that the requirements of the pill regimen were beyond the powers of mind and discipline of "illiterate Indian housewives," put the method on indefinite hold. Evidence of successful use of oral contraception among illiterate women in other countries and in programs run by some Indian PVOs, was frequently dismissed as irrelevant given the Indian cultural context and differences in scale of operation.

One of the few advantages of the high turnover among government officials is that entrenched positions on some issues do not have to be overcome but merely waited out. Thus the government has recently taken steps to popularize and increase the availability of the pill. The plan this time is to make the pill available through health workers at the

PHCs, subcentres, and urban family welfare centres. Auxiliary health workers would be allowed to distribute pills without prescription against the patient's agreement to be examined by a certified physician within a three month period. Unfortunately, the pill has not yet been approved for privately run social marketing programs.

This time around things are certainly much more auspicious but problems, inevitably, remain to be solved. In so far as distribution through its own channels is concerned, there is little evidence that the Ministry has learned the lessons it might have from the private sector concerning ways to locate and screen patients, monitor them after acceptance or create a socially acceptable network for distribution. Many government doctors still voice uninformed opinions about pills and the ability of women to use them. Which is not to say that there are not reasons for care and caution or that all physicians should be pro-pill. The problem so far is that the steps needed to provide physicians with objective, scientific information about oral or injectable contraception have not been taken. A study in Gujarat reported wide differences among physicians in both knowledge and attitude concerning proper dosages, safety and side effects, proper clinical examination of potential users, as well as views on advertising (Pathfinders, India, 1983).

A latent difficulty awaiting the pill is the vigorous opposition of urban women's organizations which, like some of their sister organizations elsewhere, see hormonal contraception as exploitative of women. So far they have objected only to injectables but their concern could easily spread to oral preparations. The Indian Women Scientists Association at an annual meeting passed a resolution opposing injectable contraception because of deleterious side effects, poor service delivery, use by lactating women and alleged "unethical" practises during field trials.

These organizations also complain of the female-centeredness of the Indian program in its choice of methods. Their tactics do not stop with resolutions and articles in the press. In some instances they have taken legal action to stop further trials with injectables and have organized demonstrations to bring their concerns before the public. Former leftist groups in Hyderabad and in Ahmedabad have taken up the cause of protecting women from this particular form of "medical exploitation." Spokeswomen like Vimala Balasubramanium, a free lance journalist, do not hesitate to list injectable contraception along with bride burning and polluted drinking water as evils that must not be allowed to continue. The Ministry seems to have taken no notice of these objections nor has it made any visible effort to counter them.

The government has, however, begun to take some steps to overcome the objections to oral contraception that are still pervasive in the medical community. A recent study in Andhra Pradesh of the distribution of orals under the new guidelines, found that while there were no serious side effects from taking orals, doctors remained skeptical of the method. Some prescribed pills for three months only and advised women beyond that to let nature govern the next birth interval. In response to problems of this kind, the Indian Council on Medical Research (ICMR) has organized workshops for physicians, so far only for allopathic physicians, to present the scientific evidence regarding the pill's safety and other information on their use. It also has arranged through 200 "quality" PHCs that have been designated as Human Reproduction Research Centres (HRRCs), to put on lecture/demonstration sessions for state health officials.

This much overdue development faces an uphill task. The medical literature is still cautionary and generally negative toward oral contraception. In these circumstances it can be expected that health officers out in the districts will not be enthusiastic for a controversial method which, when it is prescribed, will tend to pick up the blame for other prevalent complaints and cause them difficulties with their patients.

The Private Sector

Thus far we have focussed on the government's program because in India that is the primary family planning activity. The private sector has in some instances pointed the way to new approaches and it has great potential for the future of family planning in India. But, until now, activities in the voluntary sector have been a side show to the main event—the family planning program run out of the Ministry of Health and Family Welfare from Nirman Bhawan in New Delhi.

It is unlikely that the government will remove itself quickly or totally from the scene and, indeed, it is not realistic to think that it could or should do so. In India, with an underdeveloped medical infrastructure, there is no way that the entire burden of rural health services can be shifted to the private sector but there are many areas that the government might cede to private organizations while it retains responsibility for expanding, maintaining, and provisioning the country's basic health system.

There are models of how such a division of labor might work. The Government of Maharashtra, for example, has given the King Edward Hospital in Pune responsibility, with government financial support, for running the health services in a rural area near Pune. Another variant, also in Maharashtra, is the Jamkhed project which seeks to provide an improved quality of health care. A major goal of the project is to wean itself from dependence on government funding in exchange for the greater flexibility and freedom of operation. Villages are admitted to the program only if they make a fairly substantial contribution to its operation. In turn their priorities, medical and otherwise, are given serious consideration in deciding what activities will be taken up. (Jeffery, p. 284).

In both of these Maharashtra projects local groups are taken into partnership while the state plays a supportive role ranging from providing basic support, as in the case of the King Edward Hospital, to a cooperative, but essentially hands-off, policy as at Jamkhed. The K.E. project pays a price for its dependence on government funds in the requirements and regulations to which it must conform. These carry with them the delays and frustrations that are endemic to Indian official administration and govern even such petty matters as the kind of furniture "sanctioned" for their health center. A veteran of the voluntary sector and President of the Family Planning Association of India, Mrs Avabhai Wadia, has observed that

> Government grants to larger voluntary organizations . . . are fairly reasonable [in their terms and conditions] as far as they go, provided they are implemented with due speed which in far too many cases they are not, thereby causing a breakdown or even closure of work through avoidable delay (FPAI, 1985).

Some privately operated projects have ignored local government and government financing and have offered themselves to the public on a fee for service basis. This is the system in Tilonia where a group of young professionals offers medical services to villagers for payment as part of a much broader development agenda. Other projects have the backing of religious or political organizations. Many of them see health and family planning as integral activities in a broad development perspective and therefore they become involved in a wide range of community improvement ventures, including, as in the case of the Rural Unit for Health and Social Affairs (RUHSA) in Tamil Nadu, research.

While the government struggles with the problem of integrating health and family planning services, integration in the private sector is leagues ahead in working to improve "family welfare" in the broadest sense. Jeffery has made the interesting observation that voluntary projects are found for the most part in parts of the country "marked by considerable inequality" (Jeffery, p. 286). There are none in Kerala, he notes, but then Kerala also has better than average government health services and more altruistically inclined social and political institutions in general.

There is little doubt that the public would welcome a change in the way health and family planning services are offered. A study based on a sample of PHCs from Kerala and from Bihar, one of the country's poorest states, found that 70 percent of those interviewed, *in both states*, indicated that they preferred private sources to Government sources of medical care (Khan and Prasad). Many of them, indeed, avoided the PHCs altogether and obtained their health care elsewhere. Their reasons for not using PHC services are those heard widely throughout India (Table 5.5).

The study reveals other common problems such as the limited time doctors spend on out patient services and long waiting periods. In Bihar, the mean waiting time was 79 minutes, which might be tolerable if the reward for waiting were more often a concerned physician with enough time to render good professional care. All too often this is not what awaits the patient. The typical PHC-client encounter pushes the word "patient" back to its etymological origins.

Voluntary organizations in India are hard to classify since they vary in size, aims, scope, organization, sources of funding and ideological moorings. They have in common the fact that they are registered as non-profit organizations under the Registrar of Societies Act. From there on there is bewildering variety. A two volume directory of such organizations prepared in 1984 (National Institute of Public Cooperation and Child Development) includes 12,000 active voluntary agencies; a 1986 listing put the number at 20,000 (Pant). The numbers are not important except as a window on the extent of organized social concern in India. In most states and districts it is difficult to find out how many

TABLE 5.5   Reasons for Not Using PHC Medical Services

Major Reasons	Bihar	Kerala
Good medicines not available	60%	32%
Must buy medicines on the market	42	22
"Bad" treatment by staff	50	29
PHC doctors charge for services	47	4

Source: Khan and Prasad, 1983.

voluntary organizations there are and what they do. It is likely that many listed organizations do very little.

Voluntary organizations have a long history in India. Hindu charitable organizations, notably the Sevagon Trust in Maharashtra and the Gandhigram Trust in Tamil Nadu, have worked to improve the life of the poor. Under the Raj, Christian missions were prominent, with several thousand missionaries stationed in the country in the late 19th century. As in so many other things, there is a north-south divide here also. Charitable organizations are most numerous and most active in South India and in West Bengal. The Hindi belt states and the Punjab are the most poorly served.

Some voluntary organizations are essentially charitable groups that concentrate their efforts on providing relief in times of natural calamity or various man-made disasters. These were the first charitable organizations in India. Their number has remained fairly constant although some have adopted more focussed agendas.

More recently established voluntary organizations tend not to be stand-by charities but agencies with a focussed development orientation. Most voluntary agencies in India today are of this type. Some are fairly conformist; others more pioneering and experimental. Some, like the Family Planning Association of India, may conform to an established mode of operation in their general activities but, as side activities, sponsor projects with a more experimental flavor. The group of agencies that might be called conformist follow government approved "intervention strategies." If they are more successful than the government is with its programs, it can usually be traced to better management and to simplified procedures that eliminate bottle necks. Pay scales and security of employment do not ordinarily measure up to government standards so the reason for superior performance must be looked for elsewhere. It is not always obvious how these small programs can be reproduced in large scale but they are a source of ideas from which a bureaucracy inclined toward innovation could benefit.

Social action organizations are the newest type of voluntary organization. Much of the current debate regarding the proper role of voluntarism in Indian society, labeled by one commentator "the new politics of transformation" (Sethi), refers to these groups. Their social agendas lean toward the revolutionary and are generally highly ambitious. Rajni Kothari, a political scientist impatient with the slow crumbling of the Indian cake of custom in governmental affairs, puts the matter thus:

> development has led to a striking dualism of the social order, and democracy has become the play ground for growing corruption, criminalization,

repression and intimidation for large masses of the people whose very survival is made to depend on their staying out of the political process and whose desperate economic state incapacitates them from entering the regular economic process . . . (EPW, 1985, 20 (5).

How much these social action groups speak for the people and how much they are fashioned by intellectuals and ideologues out of ideological whole cloth is sometimes hard to determine. Should they be successful in their ambitions to plough under much of the present Indian system for helping the "subaltern" classes, it could, among other things, transform the perception of the population question and the way it is approached. So far, however, the challenge to the Indian system is largely rhetorical. Even the politically successful Marxist government in West Bengal has stopped short of attacking the traditional order. For the present, social action groups provide good political theatre. For now at least, gradualism remains the prevailing political philosophy.

In dealing with voluntary organizations the government has followed a carrot and stick policy. Since few voluntary organization are self reliant financially, many depend in varying degree on government support. Some are also the recipients of support from foreign agencies which, according to one estimate, amounts to more than Rs. 200 crore ($130 million) and exceeds the entire central government outlay in the Seventh Plan for assistance to voluntary organizations (Planning Commission, Seventh Plan, 1985).

However, this must be taken in context. The assistance for voluntary organizations outlined in the Plan and the government's expressed intention to work more closely with the voluntary sector are part of a recent and still wobbly orientation toward greater liberalization and decentralization. Suggestions on steps to be taken are not lacking but the government has been slow to move on them. For example, a workshop held to consider the findings of a five state study of NGOs conducted in 1987 by the National Institute of Health and Family Welfare (NIHFW), produced a set of nine recommendations calling for new mechanisms and procedures for government-PVO relations. These included the creation of a governing board that would be outside government but accountable to it. The board would be responsible for making grants-in-aid to PVOs under less restrictive regulations than are now in force. Grants would be available for providing services, for "social mobilization," and for training. Evaluation criteria would be broadened from a focus on acceptor targets to give greater attention to demand creation, continuation rates, quality of services and various support activities. Beyond agreeing in principle to the use of an umbrella organization for its dealings with PVOs, the government has taken a reserved position on the rest of these recommendations.

The government in fact has yet to resolve its ambivalence toward the private sector and its role in health and family planning. At the same time that it is announcing a new found appreciation for the voluntary sector, the government has withdrawn tax concessions to businesses for charitable contributions. There is also disquieting talk of a new "code of conduct" (Nanavatty, 1986; Deshpande, 1986) which some feel might further confine the activities of voluntary groups. Also a Commission of Enquiry has been established to look into the affairs of certain voluntary groups. Some see these as shots across the bow and as indications that the government's mind may not be settled on how much freedom it intends to accord the private sector (Sethi). Is this more carrot and stick or merely inconsistent policy? Whatever it is, it keeps the voluntary sector on edge.

It is not hard to construct a paranoid scenario from these intimations of government policy toward voluntary organizations. By constricting the amount and nature of foreign contributions voluntary associations may receive (the government has imposed new restrictions on foreign donations under the Foreign Contributions Act), the private sector is likely to become more dependent on government funding and thus come increasingly under government regulation. It would suit government purposes to have some of these groups serve as its agents for carrying out central policy. For those groups that choose not to play this game, the Damoclesian sword of the Commission of Enquiry hangs over them. The government's motives in all of this are not hard to discern. It is a way of controlling voluntary associations of the social action type. These are the groups that criticize in strong language the state's failure to address social inequities, a failing they are not hesitant to ascribe to the class interests of those in power. Officials can be expected to react to these assaults by tightening their control.

The voluntary sector is under attack from another direction also. For leftist groups, the conformist and development organizations are written off as tools of the capitalist system (Nanavatty, op cit) because by patching up its weak places they keep it going as a system. By extensions such groups are made accessories to international aid agencies that, with "their networks of patronage have penetrated so deep into the developing countries that their pressures are seldom explicit" (Dhanagera). In academic dress, these views are part of the "theory of political destabilization," the destabilizers in this case being western powers intent on influencing the course of events in India. These arguments have a powerful hold among some Indian intellectuals. Groups working to improve the lot of the poor and dispossessed are, by this theory, actually engaged in the creation of eventual social disorder. The response to this by any responsible official with an interest in preserving the status quo (and his place in it) is to fashion new instruments of control.

Destabilization theory is not universally accepted. Leftist groups, some believe, are as much concerned with having an issue to help maintain public interest and political support as they are in protecting the country from corrupting foreign influence. Moreover, many social action groups are non-political and are respectful or contemptuous of established political parties in roughly equal measure. Other contributors to the debate over the proper role of voluntary organizations in Indian society argue that government funding, whether domestic or foreign, compromises the independence and thus the innovativeness of such groups. They are admonished, therefore, to do without the backing of these agencies with their alleged "hidden agendas." This is not easily followed advice. The poor, on whose behalf these organizations are working, cannot be looked to for support; wealthy citizens sometime do lend their support, sometimes with great generosity, but in general there is neither the culture of giving nor the enticement of liberal tax concessions to encourage this group toward greater largess. That leaves the hard pressed middle class, the group that has suffered most from inflationary pressure. There seems little hope in any of these directions.

The Ministry's desire to make greater use of the voluntary sector for the promotion of family planning and extension of services faces a major hurdle at the outset: the greatest concentration of voluntary organizations is found not in the least accessible, underserved, areas but in better served states like Maharashtra, which includes the Bombay metropolitan region, and in neighboring Gujarat. The Ministry holds annual meetings of voluntary organizations hoping to interest more of them in including family planning as part of their regular activities. However, beyond convening these meeting and issuing a policy document that talks of the need for help from the voluntary sector to make family planning "a people's movement" reaching into remote areas, the government has done little to evolve a strategy for using these agencies or for encouraging their growth in under-served parts of the country.

Most development oriented voluntary organizations do not consider population growth as one of their concerns. Out of several thousand organizations only a few hundred work to promote family planning. The majority of these are of the conformist type and, if they accept government funds, follow the government model in delivering services. They adopt the same manpower "norms," accept government set targets and emphasize terminal methods. A few organizations that have not depended on Government support, at least for some of their activities, have experimented with new ideas for delivering different kinds of methods. Some have become known for innovative, high quality programs. The list includes:

The Varanasi Community Based Distribution Project (an FPAI project)
The Vadu project of the King Edward Hospital, Pune
The Parivar Seva Sanstha
The Comprehensive Labour Welfare Scheme of UPASI
The Working Women's Forum, Madras
The Jamkhed project in Maharashtra
The Gandhigram Kasturba Hospital
RHUSA, of the Christian Medical College, Tamil Nadu
The TISCO Family Welfare Project, Jamshedpur

In seminars, workshops and research papers these are the organization whose work is cited to show how successful programs can be organized and how the defects of the government program can be overcome (inter alia Khan, 1989).Attempts to analyze the reasons for the success of these voluntary programs or to look for lessons to be learned from projects that have failed, and to experiment with ways to replicate some of the more promising approaches on a largerscale, are rare.

Experimentation by these organizations has followed several lines. Some have concentrated on ways to use volunteers more effectively, others on improving the quality of services while a number have tried different schemes for integrating family planning with other development activities. There have been experiments with incentive payments, including no incentives, and with alternate modes of delivering a variety of family planning methods. Resources have come mostly from private sources including, as mentioned earlier, external agencies. Medical professionals have provided leadership in most cases but there are interesting exceptions, such as the TISCO project which has featured high quality, well conducted female sterilization camps organized under lay leadership, and some FPAI projects.

The government acknowledges the merits of these private sector efforts but tends to dismiss them as inappropriate for large scale adoption by the government. There are, of course, some poor performers among the voluntary agencies whose problems are sometimes put forward by government officials as reasons for going slow in adopting private sector approaches.

In addition to these problems at the top, the activities of voluntary agencies are not always welcome by local officials. Even voluntary agencies that have received wide acclaim may have difficulty getting local cooperation. It is usual for local officials to want to control all aspects of the activities in their districts and thus bring private organizations to heel. Moreover, high performing voluntary programs may call attention to the less than stellar performance of official district programs. To smooth relations, some voluntary programs are generous in allowing the local program to take credit for cases they have recruited themselves. Friction between the two groups, when it occurs, is apt to cause delays in obtaining official approval for projects, when that is needed, and in the release of government funds when they are involved.

Voluntary agencies face internal problems as well. One of the most serious is high attrition among their workers. The ones who remain often lack skills that are in demand elsewhere and may lack the enthusiasm of their successful colleagues who have moved on. Wages and salaries generally are considerably below government scales and there are no guarantees of security, much coveted in the Indian labor market with its high level of unemployment among the educated. Voluntary agencies assume commitment to the cause and a willingness to make personal sacrifices to it. This is often forthcoming but the foot soldiers of these organizations need more substantial rations. Finally, the dependence of many voluntary organizations on a central personality, a founder-leader, may act as a barrier to institutionalization and professionalization. Some degree of institutionalization is probably desirable in order to keep an agency locked onto its task until such time as its mission is accomplished. Inspired and committed amateurs can accomplish a great deal but for the long haul, a professional staff is necessary.

In view of the recognized potential of the voluntary sector and the great need for groups willing to explore new directions, the Government should resolve its ambivalent attitude toward PVOs and set about expanding their number, streamlining procedures for dealing with them and fostering greater cooperation at all levels of government. The PVOs, on their part, must continue to strive for greater professionalism and develop the confidence needed to undertake truly innovative approaches, some of which, inevitably, will fail.

Social Marketing

The idea of selling contraceptives at a subsidized price through commercial outlets goes back more than twenty years in India. The original concept proposed to the government was to turn the commercial sector loose on the problem of marketing and promoting condoms with government's role largely that of providing a subsidy sufficient to allow the seller at the end of the retail distribution chain to get the customary mark-up while offering the item to the purchaser at an affordable price. With condoms available free at government health centers, the only reason to purchase them from the market would be convenience or a preference for a private over a public transaction. The government contracted with suppliers of familiar household items such as tea, soap, tobacco and flashlight batteries to introduce the government issue brand of condom, the Nirodh, into their retail distribution networks. It did not, unfortunately, surrender full operational control over the program but ran it as a special project within the Ministry. Viewed in terms of the initial enthusiasm of its advocates or against the potential that this mode of distribution undoubtedly has, the Nirodh program was, at best, a modest success.

Dissatisfaction with the Nirodh program mounted over the years, both on the part of those who saw their hopes for it frustrated by government inefficiency and on the part of the cooperating corporations who found more aggravation than they had bargained for in this line of public service. After prolonged negotiations, the government agreed to turning over parts of its territory to Population Services International (PSI) India, a charitable society registered under the Societies Act of 1860.

The core of the PSI program is a force of Field Officers who cover assigned markets on "monthly journey cycles." PSI has created its own distribution channels instead of, as with the Government's Nirodh program, using those of household products companies. Every town covered by the distribution network has a "redistribution stockist" who gets supplies from PSI and, together with his own salesmen and the PSI's itinerant Field Officer, make the product available to retailers.

The PSI sales force is salaried and receives incentive bonuses for sales that exceed expected output norms. There are no bars to the sacking of workers whose work does not measure up to expectations. Work schedules are specific as to tasks and time budgets. The whole operation is carried out under a promotional umbrella that is both professional in execution and realistic in funding. Thematically, promotion of the program's condom called "Masti" goes beyond the sober messages of "prevention" (the literal meaning of Nirodh) and responsible parenthood, to acknowledgment of the pleasure principle. "Masti," a name chosen after a test of alternatives, is most nearly translated as "ecstasy" (conversation with P.G. Ramachandran, PSI Director).

PSI has plans to begin the marketing its own brand of oral contraceptives if government permission can be obtained. Also planned are seminars and workshops, conducted by leading medical and marketing professionals, for the benefit of doctors, members of the Indian Medical Association and chemists. Supporting these educational efforts would be three mailings of technical literature to 10,000 allopathic and 1500 indigenous practitioners. "Detail men" would visit 3500 doctors and 100 chemists every two months.

The plans and provisions for this new social marketing venture are in marked contrast to the usual way initiatives have been launched in the Indian family planning program. This could well mark a new beginning for effective collaboration between the government and the private sector in the promotion of family planning. The approach, with its open recognition of the joys of sex and its promotion of methods suitable for young couples, is a radical departure from the gray old program urging those "at the fag end" of their reproductive careers to present themselves for sterilization.

Community Action—The Wave of the Future?

A number of projects have demonstrated that rural populations in India respond favorably to well organized, efficiently and sensitively presented health and family planning services. Some of these, like the TISCO program at Jamshedpur have shown how mass sterilization "camps" can be run without sacrificing either quality of service or considerate patient handling. But there is little to be learned in Jamshedpur about how to reach young couples with non-terminal methods of contraception or how to work with the Government except to get it to agree to a wholly independent operation running in parallel with its own program. In obtaining agreement for a program like TISCO it undoubtedly helps if the private sponsor has the standing of an organization like the Tata Iron and Steel Company (TISCO).

The former Narangwal Project in the Punjab also suggests various effective ways to provide health and family planning services to a rural population. But while Narangwal, unlike TISCO, offered a broad spectrum of family planning methods, it too failed to deal with the question of how to mesh private and public activities in these areas. One might even say that Narangwal is a case study on how not to proceed in this direction. Furthermore, whereas TISCO could rely on the Tata organization for continuous support, Narangwal was heavily dependent on external funding and leadership. Sustainability of the operation once this outside support was withdrawn, was not a primary concern of the Narangwal project which, during its years in the Punjab, could legitimately argue that sorting out the merits of various approaches to the delivery of health care was a sufficient challenge as well as the necessary place to begin.

The Government will be the poorer if it does not examine the Narangwal experience closely for ideas that it might incorporate into its own program. Unfortunately it will learn little from that experience about ways of involving local populations so that they become not mere recipients of services, but active participants in providing and sustaining the services they receive. It is fair to say that these questions—local participation and sustainability—have not yet been solved completely anywhere in India but there are some significant efforts that may point the way. We look at two of them now, borrowing generously from a recent review (Wolfson).

Jamkhed

The Jamkhed Project in Maharashtra has been in operation for over 15 years. At present it covers 175 villages in which it has orchestrated a loose but effective alliance between health workers, village health volunteers, and local common interest associations (farmer's clubs, women's clubs). The project has its own hospital but it works closely with the Government health service, especially in training Government health personnel.

The Project serves as an interlocutory organization between the government programs and the village. It has found ways of harnessing government programs in various areas to help meet the needs that the villages, through their associations, have identified as important to them. Interaction with the State Government of Maharashtra is a central element of the Project. On the one hand, it serves both the government and the local population as a broker, bringing the benefits of various government programs to their intended recipients. As a result the Project villages enjoy greatly improved sanitation and hygienic facilities as well as other community improvements that they might otherwise have gone without. On the other hand, the Project extends services to the Government and serves, informally, as a kind of pilot project for ideas that the Government subsequently incorporates into its programs. For example, the Government sends its medical staff to Jamkhed for training and has proposed that the Project take on the task of selecting and training government health workers for an entire district of 2.5 million people. The successful use of women's clubs as a means for getting women involved in community activities has so impressed the state Government that it has set about organizing such committees in every village in the State.

According to the Project directors, the Project's greatest contribution has been to close the communications gap between the government and the villagers. In the past, Government workers on rural assignment have found it extremely difficult to establish effective communication with villagers. The local associations sponsored by the Project have acted as a shoehorn in this situation. They also establish communication in the other direction by projecting needs and interests to those who can help in meeting them. One of the most striking innovations are the local surveys conducted on average four times a year by local associations on subjects ranging from health to attitudes toward bureaucracy. With respect to local participation, interaction with the government programs, and integration of different kinds of activities, there is much here to suggest that at least some of the chronic problems of Indian development programs are surmountable.

With respect to the question of sustainability, there are also reasons to be encouraged. About half of the Rs.5 million Project budget in 1985 was allocated for social and economic development and came from external sources, plus the government and local banks. The other half of the budget was for less tangible and more expendable items: a leprosy program, eye camps, family planning, health care, medicines. The largest single source of funds for these items came from local contributions raised by farmer's clubs and women's clubs. The total of cash contributions so raised plus local in-kind contributions and bank interest, accounted for over half of the non-development part of the budget or over a quarter of the total budget.

The Jamkhed Project started out giving strong emphasis to family planning but soon learned that this was not something in which there was much local interest. Since the Project is committed to a philosophy of consumer sovereignty, it backed away from direct efforts to increase the CPR and gave attention, instead, to improving the quality of services and to population education. To improve the quality of services, Village Health Workers were given additional training and steps were taken to make sure that a VHW accompanied all tubectomy patients to the operating theater and that the Project's mobile teams made follow-up home visits. Population education was made an activity of the local community with such assistance as they might require available from the Project staff. To find family planning acceptors, the VHW was assisted by lists of eligible couples prepared by the farmer's clubs. This is the basic government program with local facilitation.

Whether the approach taken at Jamkhed helped to lower fertility is not a question that can be answered, although birth rates did decline below the State average. Demographic data collection is not one of the Project's strengths. The Project directors take the long view in the matter of fertility control. In their estimation it take three or four years of patient nurturance of the idea of family planning to bring a couple to the point of acceptance. Such a timetable is not readily meshed with the policy oscillations that have characterized government family planning policy.

Project for Community Action in Family Planning (CAFP)

This project, located in Karnataka, is focussed on family planning in 154 project villages and 255 control villages. The project villages are all of sufficient size to have a sub-centre but this advantage is offset by the fact that they are those most distant from their Primary Health Centres. Like Jamkhed, the Project works to a considerable extent through local clubs or, as it calls them, Local Voluntary Groups (LVGs). Most commonly the LVGs are youth clubs or women's clubs. Unlike Jamkhed, which was started by two physicians, this project is under the sponsorship of the Family Planning Association of India.

CAFP has cultivated relationships with the Government of Karnataka which passed a formal order sanctioning its activities. It also has developed good working relations with the PHCs in the project area with which it jointly organizes sterilization camps. Private organizations such as the Rotary and Lions Clubs, the Indian Medical Association and the State Education Council have been asked to join in certain activities as have local religious leaders. The results of these efforts to acquaint local groups with the project and to involve them in its activities have helped to overcome the considerable misunderstanding and resistance the Project encountered in its early days.

The core of the project is education. Population education is the central concern but attention is given also to health and family planning, and to more general matters relating to development. It was not an easy matter to get these activities under way since most village women were reluctant to leave their homes to participate in community activities. The Project soon learned, also, that the elected local leadership, more often than not chosen on the basis of wealth and social standing, often lacked the dynamic qualities and interest needed to bring about change. The project therefore set about finding "volunteer community leaders" (VCLs) who were interested in working with it in achieving its objectives. To prevent unnecessary friction, the VCLs were selected jointly by the Project and by local office holders. They did not replace the elected officials in any way but merely joined as additional members of the subcommittees that were established to plan particular activities.

The Women's Clubs take major responsibility for organizing various health activities. In the area of family planning, LVGs either provide or secure properties suitable as distribution depots for condoms and orals and take care to see that all necessary arrangements are made for FPAI sponsored sterilization camps. They also have taken over the educational programs from the project staff. Other important LVG activities include getting the cooperation of religious leaders and raising funds to support the Project. Support comes partly from their own resources (membership fees), partly from government funds, and partly from money making schemes such as renting out equipment and furniture to groups organizing community events, selling fertilizer and cloth and raising farm animals for sale. In-kind contributions organized by the LVGs include, in addition to their own labor, arranging for clinics and group meetings, running contraceptive depots, preparing ORT solutions, etc. Many of the Project villages are now able to sustain these activities without FPAI subvention and others are well along toward becoming self-reliant. As this happens the FPAI plans to withdraw its staff but not without first making a careful assessment of the viability of these activities once it has gone. Local contributions, now far in excess of the sums received from FPAI, are approximately equal to contributions from the government. Together these two sources cover over 90 percent of Project costs.

The achievements claimed for CAFP are numerous. Forty three percent of couples were using family planning in 1983, a full 14 points above the state average. The Project villages have consistently recruited a larger percentage of their eligible couples as new acceptors and the achievement of the government's own targets in the Project area has excelled performance elsewhere in northern Karnataka. The communities in the Project area are much more familiar than previously with government programs and know how to take advantage of them. As a consequence, government officials representing these programs make more visits to the area which, it is said, has resulted in improved services and given these officials a better understanding of local problems.

In the opinion of some informed observers, the Project's most significant benefit is the enhanced condition of women deriving from their new found realization that, through organization, they can be a force for change in the community. Of all the factors that are cited as reasons for the slow pace of change in fertility and fertility regulation in India, the inferior status of women has appeared as the most deeply entrenched. The CAFP Project points a possible way out. It is not an easy way. It will require careful planning, patient implementation and a blending of the contributions of numerous organizations, public and private.

6

New Wine in New Bottles

We have covered a lot of ground, some of it shifting as we wrote. We spent little time arguing the case for fertility regulation since that is not much of an issue in India. The government and most of the intellectual community accept the reduction of the rate of population growth as an important and legitimate national goal. What needs to be done to reduce the level of fertility is, however, a matter of lively debate.

Our examination of the Indian family planning program suggests that, overall, its achievements are not badly out of line the country's level of development. In some parts of the country, in fact, the program has performed remarkably well. Moreover we have seen that fertility is not wildly out of control. A high proportion of women, through deliberate birth control or subfecundity, complete their childbearing period either with the number of children they had earlier set as their reproductive goal or with fewer children than they had hoped to have.

On the other hand, at *present levels* of motivation and within the terms of the program's prevailing orientation toward meeting what it defines as the "unmet need" for contraception, the prospect for a significant further expansion of the market for birth control is surprisingly limited. Of the nearly 60 percent of married couples who say they want no additional children, over two-thirds are using contraception—for the most part sterilization. As for the non-contraceptors in this group, two-thirds either have announced that they intend to be sterilized—a tubectomy in most cases—or have good medical reasons to believe that they cannot have another child (ORG, 1990, 107–110). That leaves only about 6 percent of married couples with "unmet needs" as that idea is customarily rendered, i.e. couples who want no more children, are neither using contraception nor planning to any time soon and who see themselves as vulnerable to an unintended pregnancy. Such couples are ripe for the picking and if this were the size of the problem it would be a relatively easy matter to handle. Ways could be found for program workers to identify such couples and bring them aboard as acceptors. What that would require is also pretty clear, if one can believe the reasons that are given for not using contraception (ORG, 1990, Table 8.10). The overwhelming deterrent to use is concern over the health risks of tubectomy—the risks of the operation itself and its post-operative effects. Rural women are more concerned about these things than urban women but for either group this is the major reason given for non-use. Many also report opposition from elders and from the husband and some have doubts on religious grounds about the morality of birth control. (Religious objections refer primarily to invasive methods, i.e. sterilization and the IUD). Thus to increase the use of contraception among this group that has already decided against having more children it would be advisable to emphasize alternative methods, improve procedures for tubectomy and educate the public about its safety when done properly and discover and deal with the objections of those who are in a position to influence the woman's decision (overwhelmingly the husband, ORG, Table 8.15).

But the problem is larger and more complicated than merely winning converts among those who appear ready to stop having children if their fears and concerns can be alleviated. Even if all such cases were brought into the program it would produce only a modest increase in the contraceptive prevalence rate. To add significantly to the pool of contraceptors, attention must be given to low parity couples that have not yet attained their reproductive goals. This is a large group representing one-third of all married couples. Even with allowance for some subfecundity among them, these couples still constitute the largest under-served group in the population. As it is now organized and operated the program is not well poised to serve them.

Finally, about 8 percent of all married couples want more children though they already have 3 or more living offspring. Some of these couples might be persuaded to settle for what they already have or, perhaps, be convinced of the advantages of delaying their next birth. Families with three or more surviving children who want still more are most prevalent in the backward parts of the country (ORG, Table 3.4). They will be difficult to convert.

Thus the greatest unmet need, quantitatively speaking, is not found among those conventionally so defined—couples who want to call a halt to childbearing but have not yet signed up as contraceptive clients. Rather the largest pool of married couples in need of contraceptive services consists of those who want more children but are doing nothing to regulate the timing of their appearance. However, all of these groups are important to the success of the program. If those who have indicated their intention to submit to sterilization in fact do so, if fecund, non-users who want no more children could be recruited and if some significant proportion, say half, of those who still have not finished with childbearing could be convinced to space their children, the Indian program would become a celebrated success with a CPR approaching 70 percent:

	Percent
Current users	40
Intend to be sterilized	6
Fecund, want no more	6
Spacers (half of <3 ch.)	16
Potential CPR	68

To serve these different groups the program will have to change its orientation, its philosophy and its ways of doing business. We deal with these matters later in this chapter but before doing so we should note that the program of the future will have to operate with different motivational thresholds than at present. To capture a new and larger market for contraception it cannot depend solely, as it does now, on couples whose determination to end childbearing is sufficiently strong that they are willing to surmount the high motivational thresholds that the program imposes. At present the principal way these thresholds are lowered is by providing material incentives, primarily for sterilization. More will be required to gain wider acceptance. The quality of program services must be greatly improved to assuage the concerns of those who now stay away out of fear. Alternatives to sterilization must be offered for those who are not ready for a terminal method or who object to it on other grounds.

More fundamentally, the family planning program, like other social service programs in India, is in need of a fundamental overhaul. The nature of that overhaul is the subject of much of this chapter. Whether India's social service area can be made to function effectively depends on more than internal reform alone. The vitality of the economy and the stability and promise of the social system, in a word the social setting, will define the needs to be met, the resources available to meet them, the effectiveness with which these resources are deployed and, ultimately, the personal equations that govern the responses of the public to what the programs offer.

The Social Setting

If the explosive forces that now wrack the society can be withstood or released, perhaps through a relaxed federalism, India may resume its course toward the greatness that its resources in land and people entitle it. The "tryst with destiny" heralded by Nehru on the eve of Independence has at times seemed more like a prolonged marital squabble but so far the marriage has endured. The country actually did better than merely endure. During the Seventh Plan it overcame its persistent malaise and achieved its goal of a five percent rate of economic growth. The perennial nemesis, the "Hindu rate of growth," appeared to have been vanquished—at least temporarily. Some of the spurt in economic growth can be credited to the partial steps that were taken toward deregulation. Much of it stems, however, from government deficit financing and increased foreign borrowings for which the country is now paying through inflation and an astringent climate for investment and growth.

Though recent gains may be short lived and though the political, social and economic problems facing the country are massive, there are, in a longer perspective, grounds for optimism—albeit an optimism overhung endemic uncertainties and by questions about the government's ability to see through the necessary reforms. It is significant, for example, that the historical link between the monsoons and economic growth has been weakened. Average rainfall declined throughout the 7th Plan period, disastrously so in 1988. Yet the economy barely faltered and agricultural output, while affected, declined much less than in the days before widespread irrigation. Moreover, substantial buffer stocks of food grains have kept food prices in check. Whether this optimistic outlook can be sustained may soon be tested. After three good monsoons, India is overdue for a widespread drought.

Growth in manufacturing, which in the early 80s appeared to have entered a period stagnation (Alhuwalia), grew in the years since 1982 at almost twice the rate of the previous twenty years. The continuation of this growth now faces the challenge of a shortage of domestic capital, a rash of new import restrictions and a drying up of foreign credits. The government knows what must be done to overcome these constraints. To do so, however, will not be easy. The accustomed ways of conducting the nations affairs are deeply rooted.

There are additional grounds for optimism—again hedged about with caveats. For example, taken as the proportion of the population with less income than is considered necessary for an adequate diet, poverty has gradually declined, though to what level is a matter of some debate. Real wages have inched upward as have mean per capita monthly expenditures (World Bank, 1989). However, what really counts is popular perception and the general sense of relative deprivation. As one close observer sees it, there are:

> ... two currents—one upwardly mobile, frenetic and charged with ambition, the other seething with bitterness, frustration and hunger for a share in the profits—have been meeting and clashing with increasing violence .. . the aggression and bullying of those who have, and the despair and rage of those who have not affects the whole fiber of society and is reflected in their manners by increasingly brusque and explosive speech, vehement and threatening gestures, violent acts. To live in India today is to live in a constant state of tension, conscious of the explosive forces building up under a surface no longer calm and likely to erupt at any moment (Desai, 1991).

Education and literacy also have shown gains and the prevalence of moderate to severe malnutrition has trended downward. Even the much maligned family welfare program can, as we have seen, point to some real gains. While more might have been achieved in all of these areas, the achievements of the 1980s are undeniable but to continue on this course Indian development policy must change direction. Though much has been achieved, much has been left unattended. A moraine of administrative and legislative rubble piled up by past policies and practices now blocks the way to further growth.

India has a domestic market of vast potential. To activate that market, however, economic growth must continue and its benefits need to be more widely distributed. Paradoxical though it may seem, this will require that India enter world export markets much more effectively and aggressively than in the past. Most Indian economists and planners accept this yet the growth of exports has been unimpressive and has progressively fallen behind imports. In this connection it is interesting to note that since 1950, when India's exports exceeded Japan's, there has come to be a twenty-fold difference in export earnings between the two countries (Narayana, Bowonder and Radhakrishna, 1990). A sharp rise in exports is essential for India's future economic growth since, as seems unavoidable eventually, more liberal import policies will have to be adopted to provide essential material and capital inputs. The competitiveness of Indian exports on world markets suffers from the protectionism and subsidization of production that have been hallmarks of Indian economic policy. This too must change.

A redirection of policy is needed also in India's long struggle to elevate the poor to a conscionable level of existence. Poverty has been declining but still stands at around 40 percent of the population. In absolute terms this represents a staggering total of some 250 to 300 million persons whose incomes are insufficient for an adequate diet. Further improvement in this situation will be slow until the basic problems of development are dealt with. The "solutions" that have been the main stays of Indian development policy will not do for the challenges that lie ahead.

Challenge . . .

Of the challenges to be faced none is more awesome than providing employment for the large cohorts of young men and women trying to establish themselves in the work force of the 1990s and beyond. The current turmoil surrounding the "reservation" policy, India's affirmative action policy with regard to university admission and placement in the government service, is indicative of the serious and volatile nature of the competition for jobs. The problem of job creation is now in an especially acute stage. During the twenty year period, from 1960 to 1980 the population 15 to 29 years of age grew by 62 million. Over half of this growth occurred in the poorest regions of the country, i.e. in the eastern and central states. We are now midway in the following twenty year span—1980 to 2000—by the end of which this age group will have grown by 113 million. Again the burden of finding employment for these new workers will fall most heavily on the states least prepared to deal with it.

Labor is, of course, a source of wealth but only if it is productively employed. Economic growth, even if it could be sustained at an annual rate of 5 percent or better, would not automatically absorb the new workers who are coming along and those who are being displaced from declining sectors. This is clear from the fact that the economic growth of the past decade was not matched by a corresponding growth in employment. Private sector employment both in agriculture and in industry stagnated overall between 1980–81 and 1986–87 (the latest available data) and in all industrial categories except trade & commerce and services. In agriculture and in private sector manufacturing there was actually a loss of jobs. Except for increased employment in trade & commerce and in services, labor force growth occurred entirely in the public sector, a sector notorious for inefficiency and labor saturation. This road to job creation and job protection is likely to be greatly narrowed in the future as it has become too costly to maintain. For example, returns on capital in the public sector while they did rise under the buoyant economic conditions of the 1980s, by 1989–90 had reached only a non-impressive 4.4 percent (Bureau of Public Enterprise, 1990).

The protection of Indian industry from competition has contributed to the present distortions in the Indian labor force. It also has seriously undermined the country's ability to compete on world export markets. In manufacturing, for example, highly protected firms account for over half of fixed capital investment, use more than twice the amount of electric power per unit of value added, equip their workers with three to five times the amount of fixed capital and have labor costs per worker nearly half again greater than the average for all industries (World Bank, 1989). India cannot tolerate this situation indefinitely. It must increase its exports substantially to pay for imports vital to its further growth and it must make more efficient use of its capital resources. A continuation of present policies which put the preservation of existing jobs and the protection of domestic industry ahead of economic growth is not an affordable option for the future. Unless the country can summon the resolve to adopt new industrial and labor policies, continued economic growth is threatened.

This is a tough political agenda for a country in the midst of a paralyzing political standoff. The political situation in India today encourages short sighted, populist proposals and concessions that hamper the rational pursuit of long term goals. The enormous growth now occurring in the size of the young working age population together with the inevitable further shrinkage of the agricultural labor force, much of which will look toward the cities for employment, requires that the nation get on with necessary reforms. That will take courage and finesse on the part of the nation's leaders. Whether the Indian bureaucracy also can rise to the challenge and "chalk out" new directions for industrial and labor policy is in some doubt (Potter, 1986). During his early rule, Rajiv Gandhi attempted to liberalize the economy, to introduce greater competitiveness and to streamline the administrative system. The efforts soon succumbed to the ground realities of the political situation and relapsed to the populist programs that had provided his mother's political base. As things now stand, the newly formed minority Congress (I) government has introduced major economic and administrative reforms that if carried through can result in significant structural adjustment of the Indian economy. So far put into effect are a substantial devaluation of the rupee, export oriented trade policies, major cuts in selected subsidies and steps to create a more hospitable climate for foreign investment. Should these brave moves be able to withstand the forces that ultimately defeated Rajiv Gandhi's earlier attempts, many observers of the Indian political scene will be confounded.

New policies, from whatever quarter, are needed also for the agricultural sector. Agriculture's share of the labor force has declined somewhat but is still high, at around 60 percent, in comparison to most other developing countries (Chenery et al, 1986). It seems likely that this percentage will continue to decline but at what pace is a complex question. There is still scope for expansion of irrigation that, primarily by increasing multicropping, can raise labor demand. The expansion of irrigated land is not something that will happen as the result of private initiative alone since much of the land suitable for development lies in the eastern states where the most distressing poverty is found. It is sobering also to note that since 1978 there has been little increase in the total irrigated acreage under cultivation and over the last three years for which data are available it has actually declined (World Bank, 1989, vol. II, Table 7.4). To reverse this trend will require major investment and, in the case of the eastern part of the country, massive government outlays. It also means paying closer attention to environmental issues including a critical reexamination of the case for large scale irrigation projects which are meeting strongly organized popular resistance.

Also working against further absorption of labor in agriculture is continued mechanization, the conversion to crops that require relatively less labor and a general resistance on the part of employers, as in the industrial sector, to incurring fixed commitments to hired workers. To these factors, all tending to squeeze workers out of the agricultural sector, must be added the wholesale privatization of "common property resources" that traditionally have been a primary source of fuel and fodder for poor households. Finally there is the alarming rate of soil loss through erosion and destructive land management practices. This loss is estimated currently at 12 billion tons per year, double the amount twenty years ago. It represents the equivalent of a loss of 30 to 50 million tons of foodgrain production or 25 to 40 percent of net foodgrain production (Chaudhry, K., 1989). A major reason for the disappearance of top soil is the annual loss of 6 million acres of forest cover due, in major part, to the critical shortage of fuel wood. Annual fuel wood requirements have been put at around 133 million tons while approximately 36 million tons are estimated to be available (Chaudhry, ibid). Significant additional acreage is lost to water logging and salinization of irrigated land.

And Response

The 8th Five Year Plan takes note of many of these challenges and affirms the country's determination to deal with them. The main "thrust" of the Plan is to increase investment in agriculture, emphasize employment generation, achieve a greater measure of "distributive justice" among regions and social groups and take measures to stop the destructive exploitation of the environment. The Plan is based on a projected 6 percent annual growth of GDP and assumes success in raising the savings rate, holding down consumption, increasing the ratio of output to invested capital and increasing real export growth by 10 percent a year. All laudable goals; all feasible and mostly difficult.

India has always shown genuine concern for those sections of the population that have been left behind in the transition from an agrarian to a modern industrial society. To be sure, the needs of the poor are often exploited politically. Many programs are designed for their populist appeal and their potential for creating "banks" of loyal voters rather than for their ability to overcome the conditions that have kept many in a condition of poverty. By one reckoning, relatively unproductive outlays for food and housing subsidies, free meals, free clothing, and other hand-outs account for almost one third of most state budgets. Moreover, where different political parties are involved, the centre and the states may vie with each other in dispensing such favors. Nevertheless, alleviation of poverty has been an abiding concern of Indian policy—politics permitting.

Since welfare measures claim substantial chunks of social services budgets, allocations for health and education have remained relatively low. Although education and health now receive roughly 70 percent of public outlays on social services, they have tended to receive less than their share of increased spending.

A rapidly rising share of such expenditures has been allocated to various welfare schemes, including subsidized sale of foodgrains through the public distribution system, relief measures in areas which experienced natural disasters and housing and other subsidies directed at special groups, e.g. scheduled castes and tribes and handicapped persons (World Bank, 1989, p. 123).

As the country in the midst of its present fiscal crisis undertakes a transition to a less regulated economy, a course that typically squeezes the poor, it will be difficult to cut subsidies designed to aid them in favor of more spending on education or health. Some rearranging of priorities within these sectors—for example more for primary education and less for university education; more for health promotion and disease prevention and less for high-tech curative services—would help but tight budgets are likely to be a serious constraint on both educational and health programs. Under these conditions it will be essential for social service programs to become more efficient and obtain the maximum results per rupee expended. To appreciate the dilemma this poses for Indian policy makers, it needs to be noted that Indian expenditures for education and health are presently miserly by comparison to certain other developing countries in Asia and Africa. India's under-investment in human resources derives, in large part, from a failure to give adequate recognition to the demonstrated importance of a healthy, educated labor force. Not only is the social service sector relegated to second class status among government programs, it must, within its own domain, compete for funds and attention with more popular programs offering tangible, relatively immediate benefits both to recipients and to the programs' political sponsors.

To achieve greater efficiency in the social services sector, the way programs are typically organized and run must change. The familiar hallmarks Indian service programs are virtually a diagnosis of the causes of under-performance whether the area in question be education, health, family planning, or the range of programs aimed at the alleviation of poverty. Such programs tend to be characterized by centralized uniformity of design and management. They focus on targeted objectives and tend to be indifferent to recapturing costs from beneficiaries. Frequently they fail to understand the needs or perceptions of their intended beneficiaries or the constraints that govern their response to the program. They do a poor job of working with and through groups and agencies outside of their own chain of command. While they may meet their "targeted objectives" such programs often fail to make real headway against the problem they were established to confront. This depiction holds generally whether the area is rural development, education, health, or employment. The pattern of organization and the style of operation is similar.

To discuss the family welfare program solely in its own terms without an appreciation of the general failings of centrally administered programs in India would be a bit like treating a fever without knowing whether the patient had a cold or pneumonia. The discussion that follows recognizes five problem areas in terms of which the family welfare program might usefully be analyzed. These are: strategy formulation, coverage, quality, innovation and systems.

Strategy Formulation

Most sectoral programs in India suffer from undue centralization which produces a uniformity of content and style of execution that fails to take account or advantage of regional differences. This is not invariable true. In agriculture, for example, agro-climatic zones are recognized. Programs designed to increase agricultural output differ from zone to zone according to cropping patterns, water and fertilizer requirements, and credit facilities. The tendency in designing social service programs such as those in education, health and population control is to ignore regional differences in favor of centrally imposed uniformity. It is not that administrators are blind to the importance of regional differences in fashioning and executing their programs. Rather the lack of sufficiently detailed, timely and relevant information may frustrate efforts to make them "regionally specific." Centralization is also encouraged by reliance on central funding with the result that region specific strategies may be given little consideration. Even the so-called area projects mentioned earlier have followed general and uniform guide lines set by the center. This is in strong contrast to certain NGOs which, since they tend to arise locally, are in a position to evolve in ways that are appropriate to the populations of specific areas.

Almost by definition, centralization involves long chains of command and long delays in decision making. State and district level administrators have little opportunity for initiative and function essentially as cogs in a larger wheel. Even with respect to matters requiring immediate attention, they are inclined to wait for instructions from above. Population programs, adult education or poverty alleviation schemes, and other centrally designed initiatives are prescribed in uniform fashion for the entire country irrespective of differences in social conditions, levels of economic development, infrastructure, or demonstrated performance capacity. All of this, combined with the setting of targets by higher authority, leaves little room for innovation or custom fitting of programs to the needs and possibilities of specific areas.

Coverage

More often than not, new programs are inaugurated with fanfare and the proclamation of highly ambitious goals. Clarion calls to dedicated effort or renewed commitment often substitute for clarity of thought at this stage. Programs are "sanctioned" and put in place often with only a sketchy notion of their intended coverage. Questions that should be asked and researched relating to the groups at highest risk of whatever the problem is—poverty, malnutrition, dropping out of school, unemployment, risks to life and limb, unintentional pregnancy—are dealt with impressionistically. Failure to secure forward funding sets the scene for subsequent reductions in coverage or dilutions of services. Models and prototypes, if any there are, may be taken over wholesale, without sufficient consideration to questions of scale and situational diversity. Questions such as who is the target population, who is expected to provide program services, what types of services, with what frequency and precisely how it is all to be done are frequently neglected. This is by no means exclusively an Indian failing. Any country in the world could supply examples to fit this characterization.

The population control program can illustrate the point. For example, the decision to provide one male and one female worker for each 5000 of the rural population and each 3000 of the tribal population apparently has not been researched to determine what number and combination of workers would provide effective coverage. Having announced the "sanctioned" allocation of field personnel, emphasis then shifted to recruitment, to filling vacant positions, to standardization of manpower resources irrespective of local needs and conditions. The tendency to plunge rather than to plan carefully has been costly in terms of the program's ability to reach and hold its intended clientele.

It would be unfair to single out population control programs for such criticism. The well known Integrated Child Development Services (ICDS) program, for instance, covers only about half of the development blocks it intended to serve. The National Policy on Education (NPE) began by trying to do too many untried things at once. It proposed to build classrooms for children who traditionally have chalked their boards in the shade of a village tree, add a second teacher to assist and fill in for one who is often absent, provide new and improved teaching materials and educational toys—in all development blocks and all within a period of about three years. The principal programs for creating jobs for the rural unemployed, the National Rural Employment Program (NREP) and the Rural Landless Employment Guarantee Program (RLEGP), also illustrate a serious coverage problem relative to the sweeping goals that attended their inauguration. In some blocks, less than half of the village are covered and areas that have some of the highest levels of rural unemployment—Bihar, Uttar Pradesh, West Bengal, are among the most poorly served. While there are reasons for the warped and inadequate coverage of these programs, some blame must fall on a development style that launches large scale programs without sufficient thought either to the population to be served or the feasibility of reaching them. One final example is the campaign against illiteracy which has set out to provide literacy training to 80 million in a period of five years. Once again the program is spread evenly, and thus thinly, instead of concentrating on areas with the greatest female illiteracy, a group of special concern to the program.

Quality

Government programs have concentrated more on the development of infrastructure and on organizational expansion than on quality of service. Quality is an elusive concept but it is axiomatic that client satisfaction is essential to the success of any program. The preference for private medical care for a fee over "free" government services is a strong indication of the inferior quality of the latter. Public medical service, when it is available, is often rendered in poorly maintained, inconveniently located facilities and in a manner that does little for client satisfaction. Moreover, such service as is delivered is of varying and sometimes poor quality. It has been reported (UNFPA, 1990) that one-third of the sterilizations performed in Bihar involve post-operative complications. In Uttar Pradesh, over half of these procedures are associated with side effects which in well managed clinics have a low incidence. Again, analogous failings are attributes of many other government programs.

With respect to family planning, there is newfound recognition among professionals in the field that quality is important (Jain, 1989) and can be made operational (Bruce, 1989). The point here is that the forces that contribute to the poor quality of the Indian family planning program are pervasive throughout the government system and well entrenched. Tinkering with the program or crash initiatives will not be sufficient to produce a program of acceptable quality. A program that fails to provide follow up services, that reduces monitoring to a fixation on target achievement, that lacks all but the most rudimentary quality control measures, that does not discriminate among clients in terms of their reproductive potential, cannot be expected to deliver services of high quality. Even the fact that government services are provided without charge does not overcome the poor reputation they have acquired. In fact, as every Indian knows, there are no free government services. Large scale corruption and a variety of deviations from accepted norms of professional behavior means that most "free" government services are, in one form or another, paid services. Only by assiduous cultivation of higher standards will a professional and organizational culture emerge that is capable of fostering programs of a quality attractive to clients.

Innovation

The introduction of new approaches and new technologies has not been well handled in the Indian family planning program. On the one hand there has been the tendency, previously noted, to plunge into a new line of activity like the introduction of the IUD without adequate preparation. On the other hand, program officials have dallied and delayed interminably over adopting methods such as oral contraception or approaches such as social marketing that have proved successful elsewhere. Even when new approaches are finally given a trial they face a gauntlet of rules and conditionalities that keep them in limbo for long periods. Such was the fate of the venture into social marketing which may now, after years of operation under crippling bureaucratic rigidities and more than 25 years after it was first proposed, finally be allowed to function without undue restraint.

Voluntary agencies have much to teach the government with respect to innovation. Though they have generally worked on a small scale, they have had some striking successes. Unfortunately these successes are seldom analyzed closely by program officials and there are few efforts made to scale them up for introduction into the government's operations. Voluntary agencies funded by the government and presumably therefore best able to influence government programs, tend to be the least innovative. In return for receiving government funds they are required, by and large, to carry out a version of the government program in their area of operation and must contend with the set backs to their operations that come with dependence on government financing.

There are some heartening exceptions to this generally uninspiring account of government activity in the social service sector. Some health centers do succeed in providing services of good quality; there are some effective ICDS workers and there is the odd agricultural extension worker who gets out to the field with helpful information. Such individuals often go unrecognized and unrewarded, thus helping to sustain the low level of motivation that pervades the ranks of government service. It is not reasonable to expect innovation to flourish except where it is encouraged and appreciated. The voluntary sector and the private sector generally are more congenial to new ideas and those who espouse them. Thus the transfer of more program activity to that sector, with only the most essential guidelines, deserves serious exploration. There is no inherent reason why innovative behavior should be a stranger to the public sector. But, as we have tried to demonstrate, much has to change in that sector before it becomes an environment that is friendly to the implantation and nurturing of innovation.

Systems Development

In general Indian social service programs fail to look at their tasks in terms of the integrated systems that are needed to assure effective and continuous operation. Huge investments are made in infrastructure of various kinds with little attention to long term maintenance. Materials are prepared and distributed without respect for demand or need. Great amounts of time are devoted to collecting information of various kinds without adequate thought as to its reliability, completeness or utilization. In general there is a lack of useful performance indicators along with a massive burden of data collection much of which is not even processed. Departments responsible for various program activities often do not have up to date records on the deployment and activities of those they employ. Transfers of personnel outside the provisions of established norms create further confusion. As a result there are, for example, unstaffed centers; vehicles without drivers; drivers without vehicles. In some districts of Rajasthan half of the posts for female family welfare workers are vacant and nearly the same is true of male workers (UNFPA, 1990). A shortage of supervisory staff is a chronic condition in most social service areas; family planning is no exception. Failure to view the family planning program as a system further aggravates matters by assigning multiple tasks to field workers without concern for priorities or the worker's time budgets. Opportunities for rationalizing work assignments, for task sharing and for the use of volunteers to relieve overtaxed program personnel are sometimes discussed but seldom pursued.

Much could be done to make the present program more coherent and systematic. Substantial savings could be anticipated along with subtler benefits having to do with improved performance and enhanced motivation and morale throughout the program. It would not be necessary to start from zero. Some of the states have experimented with aspects of the program as have some NGOs. These could be examined for possible adoption on a larger scale. There is much to be learned also from successful programs elsewhere.

Perhaps the most promising prospect for improving the design and operation of the program comes from the installed research capacity that is to be found in India. These organizations, both those under government control and those in the private sector are already involved in evaluating the program but their role could be greatly expanded. Ways should be found to provide them with the incentive, the means and the necessary autonomy to unlock their full potential as partners in the effort to curb population growth and to deal with the problems that derive, in part, from past growth.

When the evidence concerning the performance of the government's various centrally directed programs and projects is examined the ineluctable verdict is a harsh one. The pervasiveness and persistence of the syndrome of under-achievement and mismanagement from one program to another suggests a deep set common cause. It is tempting to blame the 'babus' but it would be too simplistic to attribute the entire blame to bureaucratic dominance. That would overlook the fact that

India is a complex, diverse and difficult society to wean from its accustomed ways. But a major part of the problem can be fairly traced to the "commanding heights" from which the bureaucracy plans its strategies and issues its directives.

> ... bureaucratic dominance could have partly justified itself had it at least provided some superior technical or economic expertise in formulation of development schemes/projects or if it had added to speed, efficiency, economy and honesty in implementation. Alas, this is not so. All development schemes across the board—IRDP, NREP, TRYSEM (programs for increasing productivity and income in poverty households); those relating to the development of disadvantaged groups: children, women, Scheduled Castes, Scheduled Tribes, artisans; Minimum Needs Programme (MNP); elementary education, drinking water, rural health, housing and adult education to nurture human capital; programs for harnessing of local resources of land, water, forests—present a sorry picture (Jain et al, p. 199).

Reducing Population Growth

It is both encouraging and discouraging that what is wrong with the family welfare program and what needs to be done to correct it is widely known among policy makers. They recognize that the program is poorly perceived and indifferently received because of "poor quality of services, non-availability of staff, lack of empathy of the staff, poor management" (Revised Family Welfare Strategy, 1986). With respect to the delivery of services they acknowledge that vacant posts must be filled, that work assignments have to be simplified and ranked as to priority, that more training is needed, that conditions of work must be improved and incentives for better work performance developed, that supervision and management must be related to the basic aims of the program rather than to achieving rigid targets, that the program must be made less uniform and tailored to local conditions, that a major shift must be made away from sterilization toward temporary methods, that they should concentrate their efforts and focus on high risk groups, that the must involve local groups and institutions. They are aware of all this and much more. They know they should be concerned about increasing the age at marriage, improving the status of women, enhancing child survival, involving the private sector, doing a more effective job in population education and in communicating with the public and with potential program clients.

They have been told these things by consultants, by program review panels and they repeat them as received truths in their own documents.

The Revised Strategy for Family Welfare released in 1986 outlines an admirable strategy including all of these elements and for good measure adds changing attitudes on son preference and improving the image of the program and program workers. The Eighth Five Year Plan calls for a major thrust "involving the organized sector and the cooperatives movement in a big way to popularize the concept of the two child norm."

So-called "beyond family planning" measures are also part of the "family welfare strategy." These stress such hard-to-do items as providing educational and vocational training for women, ante and post natal care, improved employment opportunities for women, extension of credit facilities, providing appropriate labour saving household technologies. Unfortunately, as one commentator has noted, these laudable strategies generally "lack specificity and above all remain insensitive to . . . cultural obstacles" (Jejeebhoy, in UNFPA, op cit p. 131).

It is not only that some of these proposals lack specificity and may be culturally obtuse, it is simply too ambitious a strategy for a program that still must repair its basic structure. An evaluation of the family welfare program carried out in 1989 by the Indian Council on Medical Research (ICMR) as summarized by M.E. Khan found that

> . . . the quality of family welfare services currently offered in the national programme is poor . . . even in several of those PHCs where the availability of manpower and infrastructural resources . . . was adequate, it was observed that the quality of MCH and family planning services was still not satisfactory. (UNFPA, 1990, p. 159)

Others have commented similarly. Evidently the problem runs deeper than facilities, infrastructure, or postings, important as these are.

Government officials know of successful efforts in India to promote family planning. In some states the program has achieved gratifying results which show up in the government's own published statistics. They know also of the successes achieved by some the private sector programs. Indeed, in this regard, the Seventh Plan promises that "serious efforts will be made to involve voluntary agencies in various developmental programs." According to the Planning Commission:

> The programme has to be progressively debureaucratised and non-governmental structures will have to be promoted to provide leadership for the program. The program would have to be escalated into a genuine peoples movement. . . . The voluntary organizations will be associated more closely and actively with the program in order to fully exploit their

potential innovation, dedication to the cause, proximity and credibility with the people . . . (Planning Commission, 1989. cited in UNFPA, pp. 215–216).

These resolves are unexceptionable. However, they leave the seasoned observer with certain anxious doubts. Is the notion of a "people's movement" anything more than rhetoric? Will the government really grant the private sector the scope and the resources it needs to develop and run its own programs or will it retain control over certain essential program elements? Does close and active association with the government's program mean that voluntary and other private sector organizations will serve as mere extensions of that program or will they be allowed to develop their own way of doing things? Will the government relent from its fixation with targets in the case of private initiatives? Will it, in view of the fact that the voluntary sector is weakest in the rural areas of the eastern and central section of the country, devote extra resources to supporting private efforts in those areas? Finally, in view of increasing fiscal constraints, how much of what the government wants to do, will it be able to do? And if, as seems likely, there is further financial stringency, what priorities will prevail?

At some point it should be acknowledged that Indian family planning efforts have achieved a great deal. One has only to compare the national CPR of 40 or thereabouts with neighboring Pakistan which, though not too different in times past, now has a CPR about a third of India's. Even the four northern problem states, Bihar, Madhya Pradesh, Rajastan and Uttar Pradesh, do significantly better than that. In addition, an extensive network of facilities and functionaries has been established. As of 1987 there were 14,609 Primary Health Centres in operation; 102,674 Subcentres; 1,253 Community Health Centres; 2,648 Urban Family Welfare Centres; plus training centers and research institutions. Total per capita expenditures for the family welfare program, while low in absolute terms (about Rs. 13 or 50 cents) and by comparison with other countries, nevertheless have increased substantially. Expenditures per eligible couple, in 1970–71 prices, more than doubled from 1969–70 to 1986–87. Acceptance of contraception now stands at around 5 million couples per year. In parts of the country the use of contraception is approaching levels associated with fertility regulation in some modernized countries. Notable achievements, to be sure, yet much remains to be done.

To make further headway in its effort to bring down the birth rate the government will have to continue to attack the underpinnings of the fertility rate through its programs to increase female literacy, improve the health of children, provide employment and reasonable prospects for security. It will need also to take the difficult steps that will be required to increase the flow of funds to the social service sector. But in addition there are many things that can be done within present social and economic limitations to bring family planning within closer reach of those who need it. Significant gains are to be had from improvements to the program that do not depend on change in underlying social determinants of fertility. In the short run, as Simmons has demonstrated (G. Simmons, in Khan and Sarma, 1988) improvements in such key variables as infant mortality, the status of women as measured by education and labor force participation, and improvements in the distribution of income cannot substitute for direct family planning measures in reducing fertility.

There is no lack of suggestions and recommendations as to what those measures ought to be (see for example, UNFPA pp. 211–214, also World Bank, op cit, pp. 118–163). The delivery system should be developed and extended. There are numerous proposals for doing this including some that represent promising departures from the standard program. Management needs to be improved at all levels. Among the recommendations in this area are longer terms of health secretaries and the development of a separate cadre of health administrators. Doing something about the generally poor quality of service is on everyone's list as is greater involvement of people and non-government agencies. From every seminar and workshop additional suggestions rain down dealing with incentives, supervision, training, logistics and supply, research and evaluation and such nebulous matters as changing attitudes of program personnel.

We do not intend to repeat what others have said and said well on these topics. Instead we conclude with a few general observations and recommendations for family planning strategy as opposed to the tactical considerations with which most reviews are concerned. These can be group under two broad headings, one being the organization and control of the program and the other issues of cost effectiveness.

Organization and Control. It is essential that family planning not be regarded as the exclusive responsibility of the Ministry of Health and Social Welfare. Its identification with this ministry guarantees a lukewarm reception from ministries that ought to be involved as partners in promoting birth control either directly or indirectly. The Ministries of Education, Labor, Social Affairs, and Women and Child Development should be centrally involved. They should be made accountable for specific family planning or fertility related activities as part of their own approved work plan and budget. This is not a new idea but it is one that heretofore has not gotten beyond a few short term projects in limited areas. The Ministry of Education as part of the National Policy on Education has made population education part of formal and non-formal education. It plans to set up a "population education cell" at the central level and to develop new material dealing with the linkages of population to economic growth, social development, the environment and resources, family life, health and nutrition and demographic implications. By one estimate more than 100 million persons have so far been exposed to these messages. This is a model of shared responsibility between ministries that should be more widely emulated.

The Ministry of Health and Family Welfare would retain its overall responsibility for the basic health system which would include family planning services. It would give special attention to sterilization, steroid implants, pregnancy termination and such other methods as might require highly skilled medical personnel and sophisticated medical facilities. In recent days the Ministry has taken important steps along these lines. It has relaxed the rules for the use of oral contraception and has introduced new brand name pills for rural and urban distribution. It has given approval for the use of injectable contraception and has plans to introduce a non-hormonal weekly pill to be called "Choice 7." The marketing of condoms has been given a modern uplift through better production, packaging, promotion and distribution.

Beyond these laudable actions are other ideas related to structure and strategy whose time seems finally to have arrived. One of these has to do with the sharing of responsibility for fertility reduction. To the greatest extent possible, the government should encourage other agencies, particular private ones, to take on greater responsibility for family planning education, for the distribution of methods that don't require sophisticated medical facilities and for much of the research and evaluation. The inter-ministerial coordination and coordination of public and private sector programs necessary to accomplish this will not emerge automatically. Responsibility for it must be assigned somewhere and that somewhere must have the necessary status and authority unambiguously bestowed on it. One possibility is the creation of a Ministry of Population Affairs which in addition to responsibility for developing the much discussed "multisectoral approach" to fertility regulation would at the same time give special attention to problems of urban growth, migration, marriage, women's status and other relevant matters that at present are not being looked after properly. The Population Research Centres that are now poorly used and inadequately supported by the MOHFW might, with greater autonomy granted them, flourish and become an indispensable resource to a new Ministry of Population. Along with this the Ministry presently in charge of the government's program should find ways to give voluntary agencies greater prominence and freedom to experiment with new approaches. The activities of voluntary agencies that have claimed great success for their family planning efforts should be closely examined for ideas that could energize and redirect the government's program.

Perhaps of greatest importance is the need to regionalize the family planning program. Uniform strategies that take no account of regional differences in unmet need and in the readiness of the population to accept contraception have been wasteful of scarce resources. In states where family planning has been widely accepted central expenditures could be cut back and more scope and freedom given to voluntary organizations and to social marketers to figure out how to reach couples who continue to leave childbearing more or less to chance. There is little need in these areas to spend money on broadly aimed motivational campaigns or on incentive payments. Expensive, labor intensive promotion through the extension network could give way to advertising via electronic media. Savings resulting from these and other changes in program strategy could be redirected to areas such as some of the Hindi belt states where the program has lagged.

Cost-effectiveness. In anticipation of tight budgets for the immediate future, efforts must be made to streamline the program and get more fertility reduction impact per rupee spent. One major step in this direction would be to promote the use of temporary methods which could begin to bring younger, high fertility women into the program. This would also add secondary reinforcement to the idea of the small family since birth spacing significantly lowers infant and child mortality, a benefit realized in much lesser degree through sterilization.

Major conservation of funds could be realized also by redirecting the program not only to high risk areas but to high risk groups—pregnant women, recent mothers. The staff intensive nature of attending to this group and maintaining contact with them would require a reorientation of work habits and attitudes on the part of family planning staff. Some of this would involve additional costs but some or perhaps all of these would be offset by cutting back on the frantic search for acceptors to meet monthly targets. The large aggregate expenditures on incentive payments to clients and staff could be redirected to new purposes, among them being improvements at the program/client interface. The widespread conviction that the present system of incentive payments cannot be stopped or radically modified without serious harm to the program is one that we don't share, provided that the program is reoriented toward a new class of acceptors and given largely into new hands.

There are possible savings to be realized also through greater collaboration between field workers assigned to different programs. Whether or not the savings are large in money terms, it seems certain that more and better service could thus be obtained at present levels of expenditure.

Data specific to the Indian context are not satisfactory for the purpose but a plausible case can be made that, under present arrangements, private sector programs are more cost-effective than those under government control. One reaction to this belief among some groups is to prescribe a large dose of privatization. There is strong sentiment in this direction coming from certain western donors. It is a seductive notion and, at times, well nigh irresistible when the many shortcomings of the government's program are put alongside the successes of a number of private efforts. But it is unrealistic to think that the government would or should vacate this area of social service. The solution is not to be found in doctrinaire insistence on the panacea of privatization but on a balanced sharing of responsibility between the public and private sectors.

We have let few opportunities pass to pillory the government for the way it runs its family planning program. But the solution should be the reform of this program which, of course, would include better use of the private sector. The failures of government in this area and in the social service area generally are, as we have said repeatedly, pervasive and resistant to change. But there is no inherent reason why this can't be changed. One need only look across the border to Bangladesh where the government's family planning program appears to be doing about as well as the private programs that operate there. It was not many years ago when, with the Bangladesh CPR languishing around 10 percent, there was a general mood of despair over the government's capacity to operate a successful program. Since then the CPR has nearly tripled to a level not greatly different from India's. The reasons for this remarkable development are still subject to debate but it seems likely that the government's receptivity to new ideas, a capacity for testing these in the field before putting them in place and the gradual growth of popular demand for contraception are involved.

The ultimate goal is to offer the kind of family planning services that people will demand. In developed countries access to family planning is defended and demanded as a "right." That implies, of course, that the physical, economic and psychic thresholds to access are easy to cross.

All who have examined or encountered the Indian program in its public guise are agreed that in many areas the thresholds are formidable and crossed mostly by those impelled by desperation or the lure of temporary gain.

In the past much faith has been expressed in the "extension approach"—taking services to the people. However, as one long-time student of the problem puts it, "a basic dilemma facing the program is that the bureaucracy responsible for family planning does not have the organizational capacity to implement fully the type of organizing strategy which logically follows from the extension approach. . . ." (Misra et al, 1977).

This need not be. And it does not follow that the government should abandon the field entirely to others. The public sector has a permanent place in the delivery of health and family planning services. It is the proper sector to provide services requiring large infrastructural outlays that are beyond the means of private organizations. It is a sector with certain advantages in the areas of education and communication although it might do well to have many of these services catered instead of relying on its own home cooking. With respect to the import and manufacture of supplies the public sector again has untransferable responsibilities.

Where it can do so, however, the government would be well advised to put maximum reliance on private agencies. This maxim should apply equally to rendering services, providing training and engaging in research and evaluation. None of these areas could be turned over to the private sector in their entirety but all would benefit from a new burst of freedom from government regulation.

Government funding inevitably will be necessary to assist the private sector although, as we have noted, there are opportunities for revenue generation that should be exploited more fully. Some privately run family planning projects have become largely self supporting. Some have access to donor funds that would otherwise not enter the system. Some of the most useful and timely demographic and social science research relevant for the administration and guidance of the family planning program has been produced by private sector organizations or by those in the government system that have managed a workable degree of autonomy. Biomedical and epidemiological research, which is now a virtual government monopoly, would profit, as such research does everywhere, by the encouragement of a larger network of independent investigators.

The government deserves credit for a number of creative initiatives in its continuing effort to improve the lot of the poor and disadvantaged. Even when these programs underperform, they are available as entitlements to those in the population who know how to press their claims. Across India leaders are appearing who help people press their claims for services and benefits to which they are entitled. This could be India's salvation, its way of "averting the apocalypse" (Bonner, 1990). The fact that programs "are there" to be used is critical.

The way to go about improving these programs is clear even to those in government who might resist more than marginal changes in the government's role. Essential changes include directing services more selectively toward

> the most vulnerable, lowest performance groups and regions; determining the mix of services and . . . priority tasks through close consultation with client groups and [through] scrutiny of social and epidemiological data and . . . service statistics; using out-reach workers . . .; recruiting workers who will be credible and acceptable in local communities; . . . training to change work objectives and practices and impart a concern for quality of care; shifting from target-oriented administrative and evaluative procedures to team based approaches; . . . developing strategies to share facilities, coordinate activities of field workers . . . and service delivery efforts; exploiting opportunities to "network" with private service providers . . . (World Bank, op cit, p. 163).

This list of needed changes, developed from a review of a variety of sectoral programs, not merely family planning will do as well as any to guide future planning. What it does not include and what we believe to be crucial is recognition of the need for a complete organizational overhaul that would reassign responsibilities in a broadened, diversified and flexible family planning policy. Ministries other than MOHFW would assume a greater share of program responsibilities and the private sector would be invited, on terms that would unlock its full potential and enthusiasm, to consider making a quantum leap in the extent of its involvement. Change, thoroughgoing change, must occur in three interlinked areas: policy, program, and, essential for the first two, the Indian polity.

Appendix A:
Family Planning
Facilities and Personnel

The following data on facilities and personnel are from the 1986–87 *Year Book* of the Ministry of Health and Family Welfare.

Functioning Facilities

Rural Family Welfare Centres	5,435*
Primary Health Centres	15,050**
Sub-centres	98,987**
Urban Family Welfare Centres	1,859***
Urban Private FW Centres	322***
FW Centres at Post Partum Centres	467***

*Data as of 1/4/86 except Bihar and Jammu & Kashmir which are for 1982 and Andhra Pradesh, Haryana, and Madhya Pradesh which are for 1983.

**Data for 1/4/87. PHCs include 905 "upgraded" PHC/CHCs. Of 90,317 sub-centres in 1986, 56,248 were designated "rural family welfare sub-centres."

***Data for 31/3/84. Urban FW Centres include centres run by both state and local bodies.

Personnel in Position

	Rural FW Centres*	Urban FW Centres**	Post Partum Centres*
Medical Officers	6,022	1,166	396***
Lady Health Visitors	9,681	1,128	311
Aux. Nurse Midwives	56,904	2,041	516
FW Health Assistants	11,327	1,237	—
Male FW Workers			343
Other med. or educ.			686
Total all positions	102,202	6,822	3,721
Trained VHGs	393,476		

*Data for 31/3/86

**Data for 30/6/83. Excludes private facilities but includes Post Partum Centres

***Includes all medical, educational and academic personnel.

Appendix B:
International Assistance

India has received external assistance directed toward its concern with population growth for more than thirty years. Some of the earliest assistance was intended to help India develop the scientific cadres and research facilities needed to analyze the determinants and consequences of population growth, to design appropriate policies and programs and to evaluate the results. Though there has been inevitable leakage abroad of those who received foreign training—South Asia is notoriously leaky—the investment in research training has had a significant and lasting impact. Despite niggardly support from government sources, India has achieved self-reliance in the scientific and technical aspects of population study and policy.

Assistance more directly aimed at program operations has taken several forms. One extended foreign training to include additional domains of the social and biological sciences. Another attempted, during the late 1950s and throughout the 1960s when large cohorts of Indian students were abroad, to fill the manpower gap with an influx of foreign advisors. This was done mainly under the auspices of the Ford Foundation and, later on, USAID. Assistance from the United States Government and from other U.S. sources became a casualty of the position taken by the U.S. during the Indo-Pakistan war of 1971–72. Paradoxically, though total external assistance for the Family Welfare Programme declined nearly 25 percent between 1972–73 and 1973–74, external assistance continued to make up just under 10 percent of government expenditures on population. Thus, government spending on population did not increase to compensate for the decline in foreign aid; instead it, too, declined.

Except possibly for China, which does things pretty much on its own, 10 percent or even 25 percent funding from external sources is low by comparison with many other Asian countries. As recently as 1977, external assistance to Indonesia for family planning exceeded the amount contributed by the Government of that country and, while foreign funds have declined relative to the size of the Government's family planning budget, they still account for 30 percent of the total family planning budget (UNFPA, 1989). In the same year foreign funds made up over half of the Thai Government's outlays for family planning.

India's determination to go it alone in development generally, carries over into its cautious acceptance of foreign assistance for family planning.

As important as India's chary attitude toward external assistance is its resistance to guidance and suggestion from the outside. These days external population assistance funds go largely to help fund the so-called Area Projects which are, in effect, attempts to make the Government program work in selected districts by intensifying the investment in medical infrastructure and personnel. One could argue that the idea itself is of foreign parentage but, even if true, the more significant point is that nowadays foreign influence is carefully channeled and kept at arms length. One of the principal frustrations for foreign donors eager to see their favorite ideas put into action is the requirement laid on most of them that their funds be "in-budget," i.e. incorporated into the Government's budget. The highly desired flexibility of "extra-budget" funding is rarely available to bilateral donors.

This has not always been so. In the perception of some critics, the period of the late sixties and early seventies saw an excessive degree of foreign influence. The Estimates Committee of the Lok Sabha in a report released in 1972, a period when some donors were pressing for introduction of the IUD to the program, regretted "to note that the IUCD programme was formulated and implemented on the advice of foreign advisors without analyzing its pros and cons and without exercising an independent judgement on its suitability in Indian conditions and without establishing any proper infrastructure for the same" (cited in Bose, p. 42). It would be wrong to suppose that the Committee was concerned solely with the botched introduction of the IUD into the program for it goes on to "suggest that a critical evaluation of the foreign assistance rendered so far may be undertaken and that in the light of past experience and result of evaluation, foreign assistance may be accepted as and when necessary, keeping in view the overall objectives of the Family Planning Programme and the national interest ." A report of a committee of the Lok Sabha is a political document and, as such, may not be a model of objectivity and fairness, but the sentiments expressed in the report cited above resonate convincingly with many Indians, both official and unofficial.

Following the disruptions of the early 1970s, external aid again began to grow, reaching a peak of 291 million rupees (in excess of $30 million at the exchange rate then prevailing) in the year preceding Mrs Gandhi's return to power in 1980. Because of the post-Emergency Janata government's caution concerning family planning, total expenditure on the program fell sharply with the unintended result that foreign assistance came to account for nearly one quarter of family planning expenditures. Foreign assistance never again bulked so large in the country's family planning program. In 1986–87, the latest year for which information is available, external assistance amounted to around 11 percent of total expenditures. This drop in the percentage of total expenditures coming from outside sources was due primarily to the nearly five-fold increase in total expenditures since the last year of the Janata Government. In that same period external assistance essentially doubled, to slightly above $40 million in 1986–87. All of these amounts are in nominal terms.

Since the early seventies the main outlet for foreign assistance funds has been the Area Projects. These were established by the Government "to give a fillip to the National Family Welfare Programme particularly in the backward areas of the country" (Government of India, 1984). To do this, districts in 15 states were selected for "intensive development of health and family welfare infrastructure as well as expansion and upgradation of services" (ibid). The projects were set up initially for five years after which the States in which they were located were expected to take them over.

Five donors are involved in these Area Projects. The World Bank, the first agency to sign on, has projects in 5 states, Andhra Pradesh, Karnataka, Kerala, Uttar Pradesh and West Bengal. The other multilateral donor, the UNFPA, is in two states, Bihar and Rajasthan. There are three bilateral donors, the U.K. which assists the project in Orissa, DANIDA in Madhya Pradesh and Tamil Nadu and USAID in Gujarat, Haryana, Himachal Pradesh, Maharashtra and Punjab. The Area Projects, in the most recent period for which data are available, consume a very large fraction of the financial assistance provided by the five donors. In 1986–87, 96 percent of World Bank, UNFPA, USAID, U.K., and DANIDA contributions were earmarked for the Area Projects.

The agreements between the Government and the Area Project donors speak of innovative approaches to family planning but there has been relatively little of that in any fundamental sense. Essentially the goal has been to proceed, in phased fashion, to install the Government's Model Programme in each district by providing the facilities and personnel that eventually are to be extended to all districts. Most donors limit their involvement to providing the agreed upon funds and to occasional field inspections. None, except USAID, has built a staff of substantial size and specialization to work with the Government on implementing the provisions of their joint agreements. The World Bank, UNICEF, and UNFPA the other large donors, maintain relatively small staffs in connection with the Area Projects they help to fund. By contrast, USAID, though currently in decline as a foreign donor in India, and increasingly discouraged from active involvement at the field level, has kept a large group of expatriate and Indian professionals to interact regularly with their Indian counterparts. An assessment of USAID's contribution to the current program must take account of the fact that the U.S. has ceased to fund the UNFPA and IPPF, both important players in India.

As USAID recedes in importance because of diminished financial resources, UNICEF has come to the fore. Up until 1985–86, UNICEF was a secondary player with respect to family planning in India. With the addition of MCH activities to the family planning program, UNICEF has become a major player, now ranking along with UNFPA and USAID:

International Assistance, 1986–87

Agency	(Rs. in lakhs)
World Bank	1718.66
NORAD	106.76
UNICEF	1027.07
DANIDA	820.62
UNFPA	1143.91
U.K.	148.54
USAID	1080.85

Source: MOHFW Year Book, 1986–87, Table H.5. Not shown here are agencies that have contributed in the past but were not represented among the donors in 1986–87: WHO, SIDA, and FPIA.

Missing also are contributions by private donors such as the Ford or Rockefeller Foundations, IPPF, Oxfam, Catholic Relief Charities and other organizations whose funds do not enter the Central Budget.

Appendix C:
Incentives

A discussion of incentives is, at bottom, a discussion of the wider subject of motivation, be it the motivation of clients to use contraception, of workers to work harder or of organizations to outperform their rivals. The Indian family planning program has long talked of motivation and has used various kinds of incentives as primary instruments for activating latent motivation in users and for eliciting greater productivity from those who provide contraceptive services.

The concept of motivation that is implied in the way this complex area is most often approached in the Indian program is exceedingly primitive relative to the subtlety and sophistication with which it is treated by social scientists. Clients "get motivation" from workers who, on their rounds, "give motivation" as they have been taught to do in their IE&C workshops and seminars. It is as if motivation were solely cognitive and reducible to simple arguments suitable to become part of a family planning catechism. No doubt workers and others, especially others, can persuade an undecided potential user to become an acceptor by a few well placed arguments. And in that kind of a situation a few rupees or a small gift might turn the trick. But only in that superficial sense does the idea have some validity as it is used in the family planning program. Compared to a full rendering of the concept of motivation it is as an umbrella to a house.

The motivation of Indian couples relative to family size and composition has deep social roots. It should not be expected that cash or in-kind incentives at the levels at which they have been offered will make more than a marginal difference in recruiting acceptors or in holding on to previous ones. However, there is little evidence on that score as it relates to Indian couples. It has been established that the *timing* of acceptance can be influenced by the amount of the incentive and it has been shown also that disincentives can make a difference in the short run. This was seen during the Emergency when life was made difficult for couples reluctant to become acceptors as well as for workers unable to meet their acceptor quotas. The long term effect, however, was to set the program back several years in its ability to attract new users.

Early on in the Indian program much attention was given to "motivation." The Ford Foundation, in particular, made this a priority issue in its assistance to India for family planning. Not much came of it and attention eventually turned to putting in place a program than would soak up whatever motivation might be "out there" and hope that this would "snowball" into substantial demand. Presumably services that are more accessible, more dependable, and more considerate of the client would lower the transactional costs of contraception and thus lower the motivational barrier to use. As a general strategy this has merit but, as we have seen, the program that came into being was not a fair test of the proposition that supply can create its own demand. As commentators on the Indian program are fond of saying, with some aphoristic license, the Indian family planning program cannot be said to have failed since it hasn't been tried. A thorough consideration of the problem of motivation and how it might be dealt with operationally is a much needed but unfinished task. Meanwhile, there are incentives.

The Incentive System

Client Incentives

Incentive payments to clients to encourage acceptance of certain methods of contraception are an accepted part of the Indian family planning program. That is not to say that they are never questioned. The Planning Commission, for instance, in reviewing the incentive system expressed its disapproval of the idea that incentives be considered a permanent part of the program, noting that "none of the State Governments except Punjab viewed these financial measures as ad hoc and no consideration was given as when and how these compensations could be reduced in course of time" (Govt. of India, 1970).

Not only that, but with scarcely concealed disapproval the Commission went on to note that "some States seemed to favour an enhancement of the compensation amount to improve achievement" (ibid). As the Commission acknowledges in its report, one State Government, Tamil Nadu, did withdraw its incentive scheme with disastrous results for its efforts to lure new acceptors. Quick to get the point, Tamil Nadu restored incentives the following year. Since then there has been little agitation, at least in official circles, to change the system of payments to acceptors. Some critics of the Government's program have questioned the ethics of using cash payments and gifts to tempt poor people to make important life decisions which, in the case of sterilization, are essentially irrevocable (Bose, passim). Incentives have been criticized also as a source of corruption in an easily corrupted system. However, there is no serious move to do away with client incentives although it is probably true that many thoughtful Indians are somewhat uncomfortable with the idea.

A variety of incentive schemes has been tried as part of the Indian program. Cash payments vary according to the method chosen, the largest amounts going to those who elect sterilization. Graded incentives based on parity have been tried and amounts have been juggled to promote or arrest the decline of a particular method, e.g. vasectomy which declined in popularity following the Emergency. For a brief period during the Emergency a series of negative incentives (disincentives) were announced, all of which were withdrawn after the Emergency was lifted.

At present the client incentive scheme is fairly uniform in design but can and does vary from one area to another depending on the problems encountered in raising the required number of acceptors. According to the scheme laid down by the Centre, cash payments are made to clients who undergo sterilization or, in lesser amount, accept an IUD. There are no incentives paid to acceptors of any other method of contraception. As a matter of policy, funds for incentives are unlimited by any budgetary restriction and are non-lapsable. The Centre offers Rs. 235 for a tubectomy and Rs. 185 for vasectomy distributed as follows:

Item	Tubectomy	Vasectomy
	(Rupees)	
Client incentive	120	120
Meals	30	—
Transportation	15	15
Doctor	20	20
Nurse	5	5
Promoter	20	25
Drugs-Medicines	25	—
Total	235	185

Source: MOHFW (1988) *Family Welfare Programme in India Yearbook, 1986–87;* supplementary data were collected by one of the authors on a field trip to Kerala. With minor variations, all states make similar allocations of the funds they receive from the Centre.

At the district level there are considerable differences in how this money is used. Some districts provide transportation to the client and retain the amount allocated for this purpose. Some augment the incentive payment from savings on items such as meals and drugs and so payments to clients may vary from a minimum of Rs 120 to a maximum of Rs. 180. Sometimes savings are pooled and used as performance bonuses for workers at the end of the year. By contrast the IUD incentive scheme is penny ante: Rs. 9 for the acceptor and Rs. 5 for the "motivator." The total cost of incentive payments, exclusive of funds raised locally to augment the regular incentive, runs at about 10 percent of the state budget in a place like Uttar Pradesh where the interest in contraception is below average (Panchamukhi). In states with better family planning performance, it may be somewhat higher.

In addition to the amounts provided for incentive payments by the Centre, districts concerned about meeting their targets may augment the payments from their own resources and from other callable sources. This typically happens toward the end of the fiscal year when the gap between targets and achievements, if there is one, becomes clear. Funds for this purpose come largely from the District Collector's discretionary fund, from contributions made by voluntary organizations, from industrial establishments and from local government bodies such as the panchayats. At times, when these sources prove insufficient, the excise and revenue departments are asked to collect "donations" which are then turned over to voluntary agencies for distribution to acceptors. Because of the considerable power of the tax and revenue department, cooperation generally is not a problem. The involvement of voluntary agencies is necessary because Government departments can not use directly the donations so obtained. In effect the funds are "parked" with the voluntary agency while the district officials determine how they are to be allocated among acceptors. In most cases, these supplementary incentives are given in-kind, e.g. sarees, food, cooking utensils, blankets, etc.

Due to the heavy pressure on program personnel to meet prescribed targets, it is not unknown for "motivators" to spend their own money—perhaps money they expect to receive for "motivating" clients or money from their salary—on the client or the client's accompanying relatives. The seasonal pattern of acceptance suggests strongly, as do anecdotal accounts, that many would-be acceptors wait for the announcement of these additional incentives before presenting themselves for sterilization.

The variety of incentive schemes is not limited to those so far described. In Government and in the organized public sector, incentives are given as special salary increments to those who adopt a permanent form of contraception. Some states have introduced a lottery in which tickets, purchased in the name of acceptors of record, are drawn at regular intervals. Green Cards issued to couples using contraception and that entitle them to special privileges, purchase discounts and other benefits have been proposed but so far this scheme has not been put into operation to any significant extent.

Worker Incentives

The main beneficiary of worker incentives are the doctors who perform sterilizations in assembly line fashion at organized sterilization camps. A highly skilled laparoscopist may perform a tubectomy in a matter of minutes and in an efficiently organized "camp" may do several hundred. At Rs. 20 each this is not an inconsiderable sum. The sterilization camp physicians are seldom the doctors from the local PHC. The practise is to bring in obstetrician/gynecologists especially for the camp.

The workers who find and bring in the patients for sterilization, while they receive the same reward per patient as the physician, ordinarily claim only a share of the case load and, as we have seen, may have to spend some of what they receive as costs of doing business i.e. getting their quota of acceptors. Their main concern is with targets.

Awards

The Centre provides "incentives" to states in the form of annual awards for performance. As a kind of handicapping system, the states are divided into categories based on the estimated current CPR. Within each category awards are based on the number of "equivalent sterilizations"—the MOHFW's way of combining the pregnancy preventions effect of different contraceptive methods.

A target achievement rate is then calculated for each district and combined to form a rate for each state. The states are ranked within their CPR category and those in first and second rank receive awards. The competition for these awards is intense. The reputation and career prospects of department heads can be affected by how well they finish in the race. State level politicians gain (or loose) publicity and the state governments that come out on top enjoy the advantage of flexible funds which they can use for a variety of purposes. Charges are heard that the competition for these awards leads to over-reporting of actual accomplishments even though the Centre makes some not entirely convincing efforts to verify the figures. Reports of data manipulation have so disturbed the Centre that serious consideration is being given to discontinuing state performance awards.

Who benefits from these awards and what their effects have been on performance are questions that, so far, have gone unstudied. Some states have used their award money to recognize outstanding personnel and voluntary organizations that have made significant contributions to the state effort. But there is no policy governing these matters and so, though these funds have been used strategically to reward and re-enforce exceptional achievement, this is not general practise.

Do incentives work? Some seasoned students of the management of the Indian family planning program believe they may (Satia and Maru, 1986). However, the general conviction that client incentives are effective in recruiting contraceptive users is based on rather slim empirical evidence. The experience of Tamil Nadu which suffered a fall in new acceptors after dropping incentives for sterilization is frequently cited to make the point. The suspension of incentive payments in Tamil Nadu was brief so that it is not known whether, after the dust had settled, acceptance might have been restored to its former growth path without them. Similarly, the increase in acceptance at years end, when incentives are often raised, demonstrates only that couples potentially in the market for contraception respond to market signals. They also respond to the weather as is seen by the generally low client volume during the hottest months. It is not known whether uniform payments throughout the year would lower the total annual intake of new acceptors i.e. whether there is a net gain attributable to the marginally increased payments at the end of the year. It is clear, however, that a more evenly spread out work load would, in theory, favor improved quality of services. As it now operates, the year end drive for clients requires an expanded organizational effort which not only incurs extra costs but co-opts personnel and resources from other activities. MCH and immunization programs suffer neglect during these periods and the quality of family planning service also suffers. Failure rates tend to rise during these campaigns and, it has been alleged, there is even less follow-up of patients than at other times of the year. General studies of the factors affecting fertility regulation in India which look at the effects of various "program variables," have sometimes included incentive payments as a variable. The results are inconclusive. One ingenious attempt to measure the effect of incentives involved an analysis among 10 states of variations in payments for vasectomy

(Easterlin and Crimmins, op cit). Among couples who became contraceptive users (including vasectomy) over a five year period, there was a positive and significant association between the amount of the incentive being offered and the readiness to adopt contraception as measured by the time to adoption. But among the states there was no association between the overall use of contraception over this period and variations in the amount of the incentive payment. Thus it might appear that while incentives may precipitate use among some couples they do little to increase the general level of use. It is not obvious how these findings should be interpreted. Not only are the observations limited to 10 states but the payment schedule for vasectomy in 1965 is not a pure measure of the contraceptive inducing effect of the payment but, in part at least, may be seen as a proxy measure of broad social differences among the states. For example, two of the states where conditions are generally not conducive to high interest in family planning, Rajasthan and Madhya Pradesh, offered no incentives for vasectomy in 1965. Four states, Tamil Nadu, Gujarat, Kerala and Karnataka, generally easier areas for promoting family planning, paid above average incentives. Until this question can be investigated at the individual level, we are left with little more than broad impressions as to the significance of incentives as motivational devices.

Other attempts to measure the effect of incentives have been unsuccessful. Some years age, for example, the United Planters Association of South India (UPASI) experimented with a "no baby bonus scheme." This project has been derided in some quarters for seriously underestimating its administrative complexity and misjudging the time horizons and trust of authority prevalent among the rural population, in this case, tea pickers. Because of the enormous administrative problems encountered in this experiment, it was abandoned before systematic conclusions could be drawn.

The challenge now facing the Indian family planning authorities is to discover how to extend incentives to users of methods other than sterilization and the IUD—assuming they want to do so. There is almost no experience on this score. One program operated by a voluntary organization paid monthly incentives to women who test negative for pregnancy. Contraceptive supplies are dispensed at the same time that pregnancy status is determined. Performance, both in terms of adoption and continuation was considerably improved. When the incentives were subsequently withdrawn, continuation rates are reported to have held up (Stevens and Stevens, 1988). More experiments of this type are needed as are studies of many aspects of the question of how to increase the effective demand for contraception—incentives being but one of many possible schemes.

With respect to incentives themselves, it would be helpful to see research undertaken on a number of central questions e.g. What level of incentive, short of outright bribery, is necessary to activate acceptance? What kind of incentive works best, not only in terms of attracting users but also in terms of feasibility and acceptability? What do clients do with their incentive payments? Can these be channeled into productive investment on behalf of the user? Is it feasible, administratively and financially, to use incentives to encourage use of nonpermanent methods on a large scale? Are there cheaper but no less effective ways to recruit and retain acceptors? The time may come when the Government feels it can no longer meet the costs of client incentives as the scheme is now structured. At the present time there is no one in Government addressing these questions. The prospect, therefore, is that the present system will continue for the foreseeable future.

Organizational Side Effects

Considerable difficulty has been encountered in managing the existing incentive scheme. In addition, there are certain dysfunctional aspects which cause problems within the family planning organization. Districts and PHCs that are able to mobilize resources to pay extra incentives often have greater success in meeting their targets than less well off or less well organized units. It does not follow, of course, that the higher performance achieved by the former group is the result of the higher incentives. It may be that the same conditions that make it possible to raise the ante on incentives are also those that stimulate the demand for birth control. Nevertheless, in the absence of rationally derived, well understood and accepted performance standards, areas that receive performance awards are perceived to have benefitted from the higher incentives they were able to pay. This is perceived as unfair by others who may have to work as hard, and probably harder, for the clients they get. It is a major and widespread source of dissatisfaction throughout the program. To make the use of these collective incentives more acceptable, performance will have to be graded with much greater appreciation of the relative difficulty of recruiting clients among different districts and states. The rough sorting by the level of the CPR now in use is scarcely more than a recognition of the problem. Another solution would be to discontinue the awards altogether, a proposal that has its advocates.

Bibliography

Administrative Staff College of India. (1988), *Management Information Systems in Health and Family Welfare: State Level Status Reports*, Reports for Madhya Pradesh, Kerala, West Bengal, Orissa, Rajasthan, Bihar, Haryana, and Himachal Pradesh, various authors.

_____. and Management Sciences for Health. (1989). *Management Information Systems in Health and Family Welfare*, Hyderabad and Boston.

Arole, M.and R. Arole. (1975), "A Çomprehensive Rural Health Project in Jamkhed," in *Health by People*, K.W. Newell, WHO.

Askew, Ian, (1989). "Organizing Community Participation in Family Planning Projects in South Asia," *Studies in Family Planning*, 20, 4.

Banerjee, Sumanta. (1979), *Family Planning Communication: A Critique of the Indian Programme*, Radiant Press, New Delhi.

Banerji, D. (1971). *Family Planning in India: A Critique and Perspective*, People's Publishing House, New Delhi.

_____. (1985). *Health and Family Planning Services in India*, Lok Paksh. New Delhi.

Bardhan, Pranab K. (1984). *The Political Economy of Development in India*. Basil Blackwell, New York.

Barret, Susan, and Colin Fudge (ed). (1981), *Policy and Action*, Methuen, London.

Basu, Alaka M. (1984). "Ignorance of Family Planning Methods in India: An Important Constraint on Use," *Studies in Family Planning*, 15(3), 136–142.

_____. (1987). "Household Influences on Child Mortality: The Evidence from Mortality Trends," *Social Biology*, 34, 3–4.

_____, (1988), Culture, the Status of Women and Demographic Behavior: A Field Examination of Some of the Relations, National Council of Applied Economic Research, New Delhi.

_____. (1989). "Is Discrimination in Food really Necessary for Explaining Sex Differences in Childhood Mortality"?, *Population Studies*, 43,2.

_____. (1989). "Cultural Influences on Health Care: Regional Groups in India," Studies in Family Planning, 20, 5.

Basu, Alaka M. and Ramamani Sundar (1988). The Domestic Servant as Family Planning Innovator: An Indian Case Study, Studies in Family Planning, Vol. 19, no. 5.

Bhate, Vijayanti and K.S. Srikantan. (1987), "Family Welfare and MCH Programme: Rural Nasik District 1984–1985," *Artha Vijnana*, 29, 1.

Bhatia, Jagdish C. (1978) "Ideal Number and Sex Composition of Children in India," *Journal of Family Welfare*, 24.

———. (1982), "Evaluation of Traditional Birth Attendants Training Scheme in the State of Maharashtrya" Indian Institute of Management, Bangalore.

———. (1982) "Evaluation of Traditional Birth Attendants Scheme in the State of Karnataka," IIM, Bangalore.

Bhende, Asha, S. Mukerji and S. Mitra. (1985), *The TISCO Programme in Jamshedpur*, IIPS, Bombay.

Binswanger. Hans P. and John McIntire. (1987), "Behavioral and Material Determinants of Productive Relations in Land-abundant Tropical Agriculture," *Economic Development and Cultural Change*.

Bongaarts, John, W. Parker Mauldin and James F. Phillips. (1990), "The Demographic Impact of Family Planning Programs," Working Papers, No. 17. The Population Council, N.Y.

Bonner, Arthur. (1990), *Averting the Apocalypse*, Duke University Press.

Bose, Ashish. (1989), *From Population to People*, B.R. Publishing Corporation, Delhi.

Bouton, marshall M. (1985), *Agrarian Radicalism in South India*, Princeton University Press, Princeton, N.J.

Bruce, Judith. (1990), "Fundamental Elements of the Quality of Care: A Simple Framework," *Studies in Family Planning*,21, 2.

Bulatao, Rudolfo A. (1984), *Reducing Fertility in Developing Countries: A Review of Determinants and Policy Levers*, World Bank Staff Working Paper No. 680, World Bank, Washington, D.C.

———, and R.D. Lee (eds). *Determinants of Fertility in Developing Countries*, Academic Press, Vols. 1 and 2.

Cain, Mead. (1982), "Perspectives on Family Planning and Fertility in Developing Countries," *Population Studies*, 36.

———. (1985), "On the Relationship Between Landhold and Fertility," *Population Studies*, 39.

Caldwell, John. (1986), "Periodic High Risk as a Cause of Fertility Decline in a Changing Rural Environment: Survival Strategies in the 1980–83 South Indian Drought." *Economic Development and Cultural Change*, 34, 4.

———. (1987), "Family Change and Demographic Change: Reversal of the Generation Flow," in Srinivas and Mukerji.

———, P.H. Reddy, and P. Caldwell. (1982), "Demographic Change in Rural South India," *Population and Development Review*, 8,4.

———, (1985), "Education Transition in Rural South India," *Population and Development Review*, 11.

Cassen, Robert H. (1978), *India: Population, Economy, Society*, Holmes & Meier Publishers, Inc., New York.

Chabra, S., N. Gupte, Anita Mehta, and Arti Shende. (1988), "Medical

Termination of Pregnancy and Concurrent Adoption in Rural India," *Studies in Family Planning*, 19, 4.

Charyulu, U.V.N., and V.K. Natarajan. (1982), "Voluntary Organizations and Rural Development," *Journal of Rural Development*, 1(4), 513–64.

Chaturvedi, Anil. (1988), *District Administration: The Dynamics of Discord*, Sage Publications, New Delhi.

Chaudry, Kamala (1989). Poverty, Environment and Development, Daedalus, Winter 1989, 118 (1).

Chaudhry, Mahinder D. (1989), "Fertility Behavior in India, 1961–86: The Stalled Decline in the Crude Birth Rate," in Singh, S.N. et al, *Population Transition in India*, B.R. Publishing Corporation, Delhi.

Chengappa, Raj. (1988), "Family Planning: The Great Hoax," *India Today*, October 31.

Coale, Ansley and Paul Demeny (1967). Methods of Estimating Basic Demographic Measures from Incomplete Data, Manuals on Methods of Estimating Population, No. 4, New York, United Nations.

Coale, Ansley and E. M. Hoover. (1958), *Population Growth and Economic Development in Low-income Countries: a Case Study of India's Prospects*, Princeton University Press, Princeton, N.J.

Cleland, John and C. Wilson. (1987), "Demand Theories of the Fertility Transition: an Iconoclastic View," *Population Studies*, 41, 1.

Dandekar, Kumudini. (1959), *Demographic Survey of Six Rural Communities*, Asia Publishing House, Poona.

_____. (1979), "Child Labor: Do Parents Count It as an Economic Contribution?," in Srinivasan, Saxena and Kanitka.

Das Gupta, Monica. (1978), "Production Relations and Population," *Journal of Development Studies*, 14, 4.

_____. (1987), "Selective Discrimination Against Children in India," *Population and Development* Review, 13.

_____. (1988), *Population and Development Policies and Programmes in India, 1951–1987*, NCAER Working Paper No. 14, National Council of Applied Economic Research, New Delhi.

_____. (1989), "The Effects of Discrimination on Health and Mortality," Paper prepared for IUSSP Conference, New Delhi, September, 1989.

Datta, S.K.,and J.B. Nugent. (1984), "Are Old Age Security and the Utility of Children in Rural India Really Unimportant?," *Population Studies*, 38.

David, L.H. and G. Narayana. (1983), *Management of Health and Family Welfare Services*, Administrative Staff College of India, Hyderabad.

_____. (1985), *Management Needs Assessment: USAID Area Development Project—Maharashtrya*, Administrative Staff College of India, Hyderabad.

Davis, K. (1951), *The Population of India and Pakistan*, Princeton University Press, Princeton, N.J.

Desai, A.R. (1980), *Urban Family and Family Planning in India*, Popular Prakashan.

Desai, Anita, (1991),India: The Seed of Destruction, The New York Review of Books, Vol.XXXVIII, Number 12, June 27, 1991.

Deshpande, V.D. (1986), "Code of Conduct for Rural Voluntary Agencies," *Economic and Political Weekly*, 21(30).

Dhanagere, D.N. (1988), "Action Groups and Social Transformation in India: Some Sociological Issues," *Man and Development*, 10(3).

Dyson, Tim (ed). (1989), *India's Historical Demography: Studies in Famine, Disease and Society*, Curzon Press Ltd., London.

_____, and Nigel Crook. (eds), (1984), *India's Demography: Essays on the Contemporary Population*, South Asian Publishers Pvt. Ltd., New Delhi.

_____, and Mick Moore. (1983), "Kinship Structure, Female Autonomy,and Demographic Behavior in India," *Population and Development Review*, 9, 1.

Easterlin, Richard and Eileen Crimmins. (1985), *The Fertility Revolution: A Supply-Demand Analysis*, University of Chicago Press.

_____,Kua Wongboonsin and Mohamed Aly Ahmed. (1988), "The Demand for Family Planning: A New Approach," *Studies in Family Planning*, 19, 5.

The Economist, (1991), The Hindu rate of growth returns to India, 12–18 January.

Epstein, T.S., et al. (1983). *Basic Needs Viewed from Above and from Below*, Development Centre of the Organization for Economic Cooperation and Development.

Etienne, Gilbert. (1985). *Rural Development in Asia: Meetings with Peasants*, Sage, New Delhi.

Evenson, Robert E. (1986). *Food Consumption, Nutrient Intake and Agricultural Production in India*, USAID/India, Occasional Paper No. 3., New Delhi.

Family Planning Association of India. (1988), *Varanasi Community Based Distribution Project—Annual Report 1987, Varanasi.*

Ganapathy, R.S., S.R. Ganesh, Rushikesh Maru, Samuel Paul, and Ram Ram Mohan Rao. (1985), *Public Policy and Policy Analysis in India*, Sage Publications.

George, Alexandra. (1986), *Social Ferment in India*, The Athlone Press, London and Atlantic Highlands, N.J.

George, K.K., and I.S. Gulati. (1985), "Centre-State Resource Transfers 1951–84: An Appraisal," *Economic and Political Weekly*, XX, 7.

Giridhar, G., J.K.Satia and Ashok Subramanian. (1985), "Policy Studies in Health and Population," in Ganapathy.

Gopolan, C. (1985), "The Mother and Child in India." *Economic and Political Weekly*, 20, 4.

Goryacheva, D.M. (1988), *Population and Economic Growth in India*, Agricole Publishing Academy, New Delhi.

Government of India, (1946), Report of the Health Survey and Development Committee (The Bhore Committee).

_____. (1961), Report of the Health Survey and Planning Committee (The Mudaliar Committee).

_____. (1968), Report of the Committee on the Integration of Health Services (The Jungalwalla Committee).

_____, (1973), Report of the Committee on Multipurpose Workers, (The Carter Singh Committee).

_____. (1974), Report on Medical Education and Support Manpower (The Srivastava Committee).

_____, (1953,1956,1961,1969,1974,1981,1986), Planning Commission, First, Second, Third, Fourth, Fifth, Sixth, and Seventh Five Year Plans, The Manager of Publications, Delhi.

_____. (1970), Planning Commission, *Family Planning Programmes in India: An Evaluation*, New Delhi.

_____. (1984), Ministry of Health and Family Welfare, Department of Family Welfare, *Year Book 1983–84*, New Delhi.

_____. (1988), *Yearbook, 1986–87*.

_____, (1986), Revised Strategy for National Family Welfare Programme: A Summary.

_____, (1988), Ministry of Home Affairs, Registrar General, Advanced Report on Age at Marriage Differentials in India,1984, Occasional Paper No2.

_____, (1989), Sample Registration System: Provisional Estimates.

Gulati, Ravi. (1977), "India's Population Policy: History and Future," World Bank Staff Working Paper, No. 265.

Gupta, V.M. and P.M. Shingh. (1976), *Expanding the Interpersonal Communication Base for Family Planning—A Study in Coordination with Other Agencies*, Indian Institute of Management, Ahmedabad.

Hanson, A.H. and Janet Douglas. (1972), *India's Democracy*, W.W. Norton & Company, New York.

Heaver, Richard (1989). "Improving Family Planning, Health and Nutrition Outreach in India: Experience from Some World Bank Assisted Programs"; Background Paper prepared for 1989 CEM, World Bank India Office, January, 1989.

Hobbs, Frank B. (1986), *Demographic Estimates, Projections and Selected Social Characteristics of the Population of India*, Center for International Research, Staff Paper No. 21, U.S. Bureau of the Census.

Indian Institute of Management/Ahmedabad. (1988). *Study of Facility Utilization and Programme Management in Family Welfare, Madhya Pradesh, Uttar Pradesh, Rajasthan, Bihar.*

Indian Institute of Management(Calcutta). (1987), *Identification of Gaps in Knowledge, Skills and Practises of Health and Family Welfare Personnel for Implementation of India Population Project—IV*, Two Volumes.

Indian Institute for Population Sciences and Marathwada University. (1985), *Baseline Survey on Fertility, Mortality and Related Factors in Maharashtra*, IIPS, Bombay.

IIPS and M.S. University. (1985), *Baseline Survey on Fertility, Mortality and Related Factors in Rural Gujarat*, IIPS, Bombay.

IIPS, PRC (Patna) and RGI (New Delhi). (1982), *Report on the Baseline Survey on fertility, Mortality and Related Factors in Bihar*, IIPS, Bombay.

Jain, A.K. (1985), "The Impact of Development and Population Policies on Fertility in India," *Studies in Family Planning*, 16, 4.

_____. (1989), "Fertility Reduction and the Quality of Population Services," *Studies in Family Planning*, 20(1), 1–17.

_____. and Moni Nag. (1985), *Female Primary Education and Fertility Reduction in India*, Center for Policy Studies, Working Paper No. 114, Population Council, New York.

_____. (1986), "Importance of Female Primary Education and Fertility Reduction in India," *Economic and Political Weekly*, 2136, September 6.

_____, and Pravin Visaria. (1988), *Infant Mortality in India*, Sage Publications.

Jain, Anrudh K. and Arjun I. Adlakha (1982). Preliminary Estimates of Fertility Decline in India during the 1970s, Population and Development Review, 8 (3).

Jain, L.C. with B.V. Krishnamurthy and P.M. Tripathy. (1985), *Grass Without Roots: Rural Development Under Government Auspices*, Sage Publications.

Jeffery, Roger. (1988), *The Politics of Health in India*, University of California Press, Berkeley, Los Angeles, London.

Jejeebhoy, Shireen J. (1981),Status of Women and Fertility:A Socio-cultural Analysis of Regional Variation in Fertility in India. in Srinivasan and Mukerji (1981).

Jejeebhoy, Shireen J. and Sumati Kulkarni. (1989), "Reproductive Motivation: A Comparison of Wives and Husbands in Maharashtra, India," *Studies in Family Planning*, 20, 5.

Jolly, K.G. (1986), *Family Planning in India: 1969–84, A District Level Study*, Hindu Publishing Corporation.

_____. (1989), "Pattern of Family Planning Performance in Relation to Socio-economic Development at the State Level," in *Population Transition in India*, Vol I, S.N. Singh, M.K. Premi, P.S. Bhatia and Ashish Bose (eds), B.R. Publishing, Delhi.

Juyal, R.K. (1986) "Cost-effectiveness of Family Planning in India: The Longrun Average and Marginal Costs," *Health Policy and Planning*, 1, 2.

Jobert, Bruno. (1985), "Populism and Health Policy: The Case of Community Health Volunteers," *Social Science and Medicine*, 20, 1.

Kanitkar, T. and B.N. Murthy. (1988), "Factors Associated with Contraception in Bihar and Rajasthan: Findings from Recent Sample Surveys," in Srinivasan and Mukerji.

Kantner, John. (1986), *Population in India's Development*, USAID/India, Occasional Paper No.1, New Delhi.

Kapoor, P.N. (1989), "Recent Decline in Birth Rate in India and its Relationship with Contraceptive Prevalence," in *Population Transition in India*, S.N. Singh et al (eds.), B.R. Publishing Corporation, Vol. 1.

Karve, I. (1965), *Kinship Organization in India*, Asia Publishing House Bombay.

Khan, M.E., (1988), India Population Project II in Uttar Pradesh, Operations Research Group, Baroda.

_____, (1989), *Experiences of NGO's and Organized Sector in Family Planning—Some Selected Observations*, Operations Research Group, Baroda. See also UNFPA, 1990.

_____. et al. (1983), "Women and Health—A Case Study of Sex Discrimination," Paper presented to ICMR/Ford Foundation Workshop on Child Health, Nutrition and Population.

_____ and R.B. Gupta. (1988), *Community Participation in Family Planning: A Case Study of the Kundam Family Welfare Project*, IPPF, London.

_____ and C.V.S. Prasad. (1980), *Family Planning Practises—Second All India Survey*, Operations Research Group, Baroda.

_____. (1983). Family Planning Practices in India—Second All India Survey, Operations research Group, Baroda.

_____. (1985), "A Comparison of 1970 and 1980 Survey Findings on Family Planning in India," *Studies in Family Planning*, 16, No. 6.

_____. (1983), "What Inhibits Indian Couples Not Wanting More Children from Using Family Planning?," *Studies in Population Health and Family Planning: Working Papers"*, Operations Research Group, Baroda.

_____ and Sandhyo Rao. (1989), "Do Welfare Services Reach Couples Below the Poverty Line? A Case Study of Family Welfare Programme in Bihar", in *Population Transition in India*, S.N. Singh et al (eds), B.R. Publishing Corporation, Vol. 2.

_____ and D.V.N. Sarma (1988). Socio-economic Development and Population Control, Manohar, New Delhi.

Kielmann, A. and Associates. (1983), *Childhood and Maternal Health Services in Rural India, The Narangwal Experiment:* Vol I, Johns Hopkins University Press.

Kohli, Atul. (1987), *The State and Poverty in India: The Politics of Reform*, Cambridge University Press, Cambridge, New York, Melbourne.

_____, (1989), Politics of Economic Liberalization in India, World Development, Vol. 17, No.3.

Kothari, Rajni. (1985), "The Non-Party Political Process". *Economic and Political Weekly*, 20(5), 216–224.

Krishnamurthy, S. (1979), "Mortality Level, Desire for Surviving Sons and Rate of Population Increase", *Population Studies*, 33, 3.

Krishnan, T.N. (1976), "Demographic Transition in Kerala: Facts and Factors," *Economic and Political Weekly*, Special No. XI, Numbers 30–33.

Lahiri, Subrata, (1984), Demand for Sons Among Indian Couples by Urban-Rural Settlement Size, Demography India, 13,1.

Lannoy, Richard. (1975), *The Speaking Tree*, Oxford University Press, New York.

Lapham, R. and W.P. Mauldin. (1985), "Contraceptive Prevalence: The Influence of Organized Family Programs," *Studies in Family Planning*, 16, 3.

_____. (1987), "The Effects of Family Planning on Fertility: Research Findings," In R.J. Lapham and G.B. Simmons, (eds), *Organizing for Effective Family Planning Programs*, National Academy Press, Washington, D.C.

Lapham, R.J. and George Simmons (eds). (1987), *Organizing for Effective Family Planning Programs*, National Academy Press.

Lloyd, C. and J. Ross. (1989), "Methods for Measuring the Fertility Impact of Family Planning Programs: The Experience of the Last Decade," Working Papers No 7, The Population Council.

Maheshwari, Shriram. (1984), "Administrating the Planning System," *Indian Journal of Public Administration*, xxx, 3.

Mamdani, Mahmood. (1972), *The Myth of Population Control: Family, Caste and Class in an Indian Village*, Monthly Review Press.

Mandlebaum, D. (1986), "Sex Roles and Gender Relations in North India," *Economic and Political Weekly*, 21.

Mankekar, Kamala. (1974), *Voluntary Efforts in Family Planning—A Brief History*, Abhiman Publications, New Delhi.

Maru, Rishikesh. (1985), "Policy Formation as a Political Process, A Case Study of Health Manpower: 1949-75," in Ganapathy.

_____, Nirmala Murthy and Ashok Subramanian. (1983), *A Report of the Workshop on Management Issues in Voluntary Organizations*, Indian Institute of Management, Ahmedabad.

Mauldin, W.P. and Sheldon Segal. (1986), *Prevalence of Contraceptive Use in Developing Countries*, The Rockefeller Foundation, New York.

Mellor, John W. (1976), *The New Economics of Growth: a Strategy for India and the Developing World*, a Twentieth Century Fund Study, Cornell University Press, Ithaca, New York.

_____. (1988). "Food Production, Consumption and Development Strategy," in *The Indian Economy*, Robert E.B. Lucas and Gustav F. Papanek (eds). Oxford University Press.

Meltzner, Arnold J. (1976), *Policy Analysis in the Bureaucracy*, University of California Press, Berkeley.

Midgley, J. (1986), *Community Participation, Social Development and the State*, Methuen & Co., London.

Miller, B.D. (1981), *The Endangered Sex: Neglect of Female Children in North India*, Cornell University Press.

Miller, B. (1989), "Changing Patterns of Juvenile Sex Ratios in Rural India: 1961-71," Economic and Political Weekly, 24, 22.

Mishra, Bhasker D., Ali Sharif, Ruth Simmons and George B. Simmons, (1982) *Organization for Change: A Systems Analysis of Family Planning in India*, Radiant Publishers, New Delhi.

Mitra, Ashok. (1978), *India's Population: Aspects of Quality and Control*, Abhinay Publications, New Delhi.

Mosley, W. Henry and Lincoln Chen. (1984), "An Analytical Framework for the Study of Child Survival in Developing Countries," in Mosley and Chen (eds), *Child Survival: strategies for research, Population and Development Review,* a supplement to Vol. 10.

Murthy, Nirmala. (1986), "Family Planning Programs: Lessons from Management Interventions," *Vikalpa,* 11,3, 205–214.

Murthy, A.K. Srinivas and R.L. Parker. (1973), "New Methods for Assessing Health Care Delivery Systems," *Indian Journal of Medical Education,* 12, 3 & 4, 269–277.

Nag, Moni. (1980). "How Modernization Can Also Increase Fertility," *Current Anthropology,* Vol. 21, No. 5.

_____. (1985), "Sociocultural Factors Affecting the Cost of Fertility Regulation," *Population Bulletin,* 17, United Nations.

_____. (1986). "Why People Desiring Birth Control Still Do Not Use Contraception," *Populi,* 13.

_____, and N. Kak. (1984), "Demographic Transition in a Punjab Village," *Population and Development Review,* 10.

Naik, J.P. (ed). (1977), *Alternative System of Health Care Services in India,* Indian Council of Social Science Research.

Namboodiri, N.K. (1972), "Some Observations on the Economic Framework of Fertility," *Population Studies,* 26, 185–206.

Nanavatty, Meher C. (1986), "Voluntary Sector in Historical Perspective," *Mainstream,* 24(45), 20.

Narayana, G. (1980), "Problems of Caste in Development Administration: A Study of Health and Family Welfare Workers in Karnataka," *Emerging Sociology,* 4, 103–114.

_____. (1981), "Field Workers in Health and Family Planning: A Review, *ASCI Journal of Management,* 10,2, 138–148.

_____. (1982), "Job Analysis and Workload Assessment of Female Workers in India", *ASCI Journal of Management,* 11, 2, 99–109.

_____. (1983), "Reorganization of Health and Family Welfare Department in Karnataka State—The Role of Consultants," ICOMP, Kaula Lumpur.

_____. (1984), "Incentives in Family Planning Programs: Some Reflections on Theory and Practise," Administrative Staff College of India, Hyderabad.

_____, and J. Acharaya, (1980), *Problems of Field Workers: Study of Eight Primary Health Centres in Four States,* Administrative Staff College of India, Hyderabad.

_____, and V. Pandey. (1987), *Community Communications Networks and Family Planning Practises in Andhra Pradesh,* Administrative Staff College of India, Hyderabad.

_____, B. Bowonder and Radhakrishna (1990). Civil Service in India: Human Resource Development Needs, Administrative Staff College of India, Hyderabad (mimeo).

Neale, Walter C. (1985), "Indian Community Development, Local Government, Local Planning, and Rural Policy since 1950," *Economic Development and Cultural Change,* 33, July, 1985.

Ness, G.D., and H. Ando. (1984), *The Land is Shrinking: Population Planning in Asia*, The Johns Hopkins University Press.

Ness, Gayl, Timothy Johnson and Stan Bernstein (1988). Assessment of Asian Family Planning Program Performance, USAID, Report No 2. Washington.

Nortman, Dorothy L. (1985), *Population and Family Planning*, 12th Edition, Population Council, New York.

Operations Research Group. (ORG),(1988), *India Population Project II in Uttar Pradesh*, Baroda.

————,Family Planning Practices in India:Third All India Survey,Vol.II, Baroda, 1990.

Palloni, Alberto. (1987), "Theory, Analytical Frameworks and Causal Approach in the Study of Mortality at Young Ages in Developing Countries," Ann.Soc.Belge Med.Trop.67,Suppl.1, 31–45.

Panandiker, V.A. Pai, R.N. Bishnoi and O.P. Sharma. (1983), *Organizational Policy for Family Planning*, Uppal Publishing House, New Delhi.

————, and A. Sud. (1978), *Public Sector as an Instrument of Development*, Indian Council of Social Science Research.

Panchamukhi, P.R. *Aspects of Financing Population and Health in India: The Seventh Plan Perspective*, Indian Institute of Education, Pune. (no date).

Pandey, G.D. and P.P. Talwar. (1987), "Some Aspects of Marriage and Fertility in Rural Uttar Pradesh," *Demography India*, 16, 2.

Pandey, U. (1988), *Kasturba Gandhi Hospital—Gandhigram*. Administrative Staff College of India, Hyderabad.

Pant, Niranjan. (1986), *PVOs in India*, USAID, New Delhi.

Panchamuki, P.R. *Aspects of Financing Population and Health in India: The Seventh Plan Perspective*, Indian Institute of Education, Pune.

Pathfinders. (1983), *Qualitative Research on Contraceptives—Gujarat*, Pathfinders: India, Bombay.

Population Council. (1987), *Population Policies and Programs in India*, Consultant's Report to USAID, The Population Council, New York.

Prabhavathy, K. and A. Shenshadri. (1987), "Pattern of IUD Use: Follow-up of Acceptors in Mysore," *Journal of Family Welfare*.

Preston, Samuel H. and P.N. Mari Bhat. (1984), "New Evidence on Fertility and Mortality Trends in India," *Population and Development Review*, 10, 3.

Public Systems Group. (1985), *Study of Facility Utilization and Programme Management in Family Welfare—Madhya Pradesh*, Indian Institute of management, Ahmedabad.

————. (1985), *Study of Facility Utilization and Programme Management in Family Welfare—Rajasthan*, Indian Institute of Management, Ahmedabad.

————. (1985), *Study of Facility Utilization and Programme Management in Family Welfare—Bihar*, Indian Institute of Management, Ahmedabad.

Rao, N. Rama, J.R. Rele and James A. Palmore. (1987), *Regression Estimates of Fertility for India: 1971 and 1981*, Occasional Paper No. 3, Office of Registrar General & Census Commissioner, India.

Rao, T.V. (1977), *A Study of Worker-Client Transactions*, Indian Institute of Management, Ahmedabad.

Rao, V.K.R.V. (1976), "Some Thoughts on Social Change in India," in Srinivas et al, *Dimensions of Social Change in India*, Allied Publishers Private Ltd. New Delhi.

Reddy, I.U.B. (1987), "Role of Voluntary Agencies in Rural Development," *The Indian Journal of Public Administration*, 33, 3.

Reddy, P.H. and G. Narayana. (1977), "Health and Family Welfare Programme Personnel—A Study of Job Satisfaction," *Newsletter*, Population Centre, Bangalore.

Rele, J.R., (1987), "Fertility Levels and Trends in India: 1951–81," *Population and Development Review*, 13, 3, The Population Council.

Rogers, Gerry (ed). (1989), *Population Growth and Poverty in Rural South Asia*, Sage Publishers.

_____, S. Gupta, A.N. Sharma, and B. Sharma. (1989), "Demographic Patterns and Poverty among Households in Rural Bihar," in Rogers.

Rondinelli, Dennis A. and J.R. Nellis. (1986), "Assessing Decentralization Policies in Developing Countries: The Case for Cautious Optimism," *Development Policy Review*, 4.

Rosenzweig, M.R. and Robert Evenson, (1977), Fertility, Schooling, and Economic Contribution of Children in Rural India: an econometric analysis, Econometrica, 45.

Rosenzweig, N.R., and T. Schultz. (1982), "Market Opportunities, Genetic Endowments and the Intra-family Distribution of Resources: Child Survival in Rural India," *American Economic Review*, Sept.

Roy, Sanjit. (1986), "The Tilonia Model—A New Approach to Cooperative Development," Social Work Research Centre, Tilonia, Rajasthan, (mimeo).

Satia, J.K. (1983), "Cost Benefit and Effectiveness Analysis Experiences in Indian Family Planning Programs," in Sirageldin (ed), *Evaluating Population Programs*, Croom Helm, London.

_____, N. Murthy, R. Maru abd H,N, Pathak. (1985), *Strategy Formulation for Family Welfare Programme*, Indian Institute of Management, Ahmedabad.

_____, and Rishikesh Maru. (1986), "Incentives and Disincentives in the Indian Family Planning Programme," *Studies in Family Planning*, 17(3), 136–145.

_____, and G. Giridhar,(1990),Supply Aspects of Meeting Demand for Family Planning, in UNFPA, 1990.

Sawhney, Nirmal. ( ), *Multi-Purpose Concept at District Level: An Evaluation Report*, Lucknow Population Centre.

Seckler, Daniel and R.K. Sampath. (1986), *Production and Poverty in Indian Agriculture*, USAID/India, Occasional Paper Series, No. 1. New Delhi.

Sethi, H. (1985), "The Immortal Other—Debate Between Party and Non-Party Groups," *Economic and Political Weekly*, 20, 8.

_____. (1984), "Groups in a New Politics of Transformation," *Economic and Political Weekly*, 19(7), 305–316.

Singh, Harbans. ((1990), "India's High Fertility Despite Family Planning: an Appraisal," In *Population Policy: Contemporary Issues*, Godfrey Roberts, (ed), Praeger, N.Y. and London.

Singh, S.N., M.K. Premi, P.S. Bhatia and Ashish Bose (1989), *Population Transition in India*, B.R. Publishing House, Delhi.

Soni, Veena. (1983), "Thirty Years of the Indian Family Planning Program: Past Performance, Future Prospects," *International Family Planning Perspectives*, Vol.9, No.2.

Sopher, David (ed). (1980), *An Exploration of India: Perspectives on Society and Culture*, Cornell University Press.

_____. (1980), "The Geographical Patterning of Culture in India," in Sopher.

Srikantan, K. Sivaswamy and K. Balasubramanian. (1989), "Stalling of Fertility Decline in India," in *Population Transition in India*, S.N. Singh et al (eds), B.R. Publishing Corporation, Delhi.

Srinivas, M.N., (1977), Culture and Human Fertility in India, Oxford University Press, Bombay.

Srinivas, M.N. and E.A. Ramaswamy. (1977), *Culture and Human Fertility in India*, Oxford University Press, New Delhi.

_____, S. Seshaiah and V.S. Parthasarathy,(eds.), (1976), *Dimensions of Social Change in India*, Allied Publishers Private Limited, New Delhi.

Srinivasan, K. (1987), "An Analytical Note on Recent Trends in Fertility, Contraceptive Use and Infant Mortality in India," Indian Institute for Population Sciences, Bombay, (mimeo).

_____. (1988), "Modernization, Contraception, and Fertility Change in India," *International Family Planning Perspectives*, 14, 3.

_____. (1989), "Natural Fertility and Nuptiality Patterns in India," in *Population Transition in India*, B.R. Publishing Corporation, Delhi.

_____. (1990), "Determinants of Breastfeeding and Post Partum Amenorrhea in Orissa: A Hazard Model Analysis," Social Biology, (forthcoming).

_____, Shireen J. Jejeebhoy, (1981), Changes in Natural Fertility in India, 1959–1972, in Srinivasan and Mukerji, 1981.

_____. Shireen J. Jejeebhoy, Richard Easterlin and Eileen M. Crimmins. (1984), "Factors Affecting Fertility Control in India," *Population and Development Review*, 10, 2.

_____, and S. Mukerji, (eds), Dynamics of Population and Family Welfare, Himalaya Publ. House.

_____.(1987), *Dynamics of Population and Family Welfare, 1987*, Himalaya Publ. House.

_____. P.H. Reddy and V.M.N. Raju. (1978), "From One Generation to the Next: Changes in Fertility, Family Size Preference and Family Planning in an Indian State between 1951 and 1975," Studies in Family Planning, 10, 11.

_____. K. Roy and S. Ghogale. (1980), *Family Planning Targets by States for India, Vol. 1, Methodology and Input Data*, International Institute for Population Sciences, Bombay.

_____. P.C. Saxena and T. Kanitkar (eds). (1979), *Demographic and Socio-economic Aspects of the Child in India*, Himalaya Publishing House.

Stout, Susan. (1988), *Changing the Signals*, World Bank, AS4PW.

United Nations. (1961), *The Mysore Population Study*, Department of Economic and Social Affairs.

_____. (1982), *Population of India*, Country Monograph Series No. 10, ESCAP, United Nations.

_____. (1984), *Report of the International Conference on Population*, United nations: New York.

_____. (1989), "Levels and Trends of Contraceptive Use," *Population Studies*, No. 110, New York.

UNFPA, Global Population Assistance Report 1982–1988, New York,1989.

_____, South Asia Study of Population Policy and Programmes:India, New Delhi, 1990.

_____, IPPF, and the Population Council, (1981), *Family Planning in the 1980s*, Population Council: New York.

Vaidyanathan, A. (1988), "Agricultural Development and Rural Poverty," in *The Indian Economy: Recent Developments and Future Prospects*, Robert E.B. Lucas and Gustav F. Papanek, (eds), Oxford University Press, Delhi.

Visaria, Leela. (1985), "Infant Mortality in India: Level, Trends and Deteminants," *Economic and Political Weekly*, 20, 34.

_____. (1988), "Sex Differentials in Nutritional Status and Survival during Infancy and Childhood: A review of Available Evidence," IUSSP Conference paper, Asker, Norway.

Visaria, P.M. (1969), "Mortality and Fertility in India: 1951–1961," *Milbank Memorial Fund Quarterly*, 47, 1.

_____. (1971), *The Sex Ratio of the Population of India*, Census Monograph Number 10, Office of Registrar General.

Vlassoff, C. (1990), "The Value of Sons in an Indian Village: How Widows See It," *Population Studies*, 44, 5.

_____. (1990), "Fertility Intentions and Subsequent Behavior: A Longitudinal Study in Rural India," *Studies in Family Planning*, 21, 4.

Vlassoff, M. (1979), "Labour Demand and Economic Utility of Children: A Case Study in Rural India," *Population Studies*, 34.

_____. (1982), "Economic Utility of Children and Fertility in Rural India," Population Studies, 36.

_____. (1984), "Old Age Security and the Utility of Children in Rural India: A Rejoinder to Datta dn Nuggent," *Population Studies*, 38.

Vlassoff, M. and Vlassoff, C. (1980). "Old Age Security and the Utility of Children in Rural India," *Population Studies*, 34.

Wadia, Avabai. (1984), *The Family Planning Programme in India The Non-Government Sector*, Family Planning Association of India, Bombay.

Warwick, Donald P. (1988), "Culture and Management of Family Planning Programs," *Studies in Family Planning*, 19(1).

Warwick, Donald (1986). The Indonesian Family Planning Program: Government Influence and Client Choice, Population and Development Review, 12, 3.

Wolfson, Margaret. (1987), *Community Action for Family Planning*, Development Centre of the OECD, Paris.

World Bank. (1984), *World Development Report 1984*.

_____. (1989), *India, Poverty, Employment and Social Service*, Report No 7617-N. Two Volumes.

Wyon, John B. and John E. Gordon. (1971), *The Khanna Study*, Harvard University Press, Cambridge, Mass.

Zachariah, K.C. and Sulekha Patel. (1984), *Determinants of Fertility Decline in India*, World Bank Staff Working Papers, No. 699.

Index